THE SEA, THE SKY AND DUBLIN PORT

The Sea, the Sky and Dublin Port

Ian Elliott

(edited by Peigin Doyle)

Wordwell

First published in 2022
Wordwell Ltd
Unit 9, 78 Furze Road, Sandyford Industrial Estate, Dublin 18
www.wordwellbooks.com

ISBN 978-1-913934-75-0

British Library Cataloguing-in-Publication Data.
A catalogue record for this book is available from the British Library.

Note: Every effort had been made to identify the source or owners of images used in this book but in some cases this was not possible. Where images are subsequently identified corrections will be made in a later edition.

Typeset in Ireland by Wordwell Ltd
Index: Peigin Doyle
Picture research: Marta Lopez
Cover design and artwork: Wordwell Ltd
Printed by Gráficas Castuera, Pamplona

Contents

Editor's preface

When Ian Elliott wrote this book on the development of Dublin port, his vast knowledge as a scientist and astrophysicist allowed him to set the story of the port's growth and its expansion downriver towards the sea within the context of the great scientific and technological advances of the last four centuries.

Dublin was an unlikely location in which an important trading port might develop. It was tidal, with a meandering river channel, girded by dangerous sand banks at its mouth, exposed and buffeted by treacherous easterly winds.

And yet. It sat on the east coast of the country facing to the then Viking and continental worlds, close to busy trade routes on Europe's Atlantic shore. At the same time, it gave access to the heart of the country. Dublin became a trading hub for the Vikings, an administrative centre under the Anglo-Normans and English. Stone and other materials were imported to construct the new churches and buildings of the growing town. Craftspeople and other settlers followed. Through the centuries the produce of the country was traded through the port and essentials and luxury goods imported in return. Without its port, the city could not have thrived.

Later, amid wider intellectual developments, dedicated and far-sighted port engineers drove the port's growth.

Up to the late eighteenth century, many boats made first landing at the Poolbeg peninsula where deep water at 'the Rings' End' gave sheltered berths. Cargoes and passengers were transferred to lighter boats that could travel upriver into the heart of the town where, in 1707 the first Custom House for the port was built at Wellington Quay. Quays were built to contain the river on either side creating more berths for the growing traffic. Protective sea walls snaked upriver from the sandbanks and downriver from the city.

All this time, scientists were searching for an accurate way of telling the time. This was essential to enable navigators to calculate their speed and distance travelled and, so, their location out at sea. The passage of the Sun, Moon and planets were all tracked by astronomers to measure the passing of time. Astronomers at Dunsink Observatory north of Dublin played a significant part in helping mariners at Dublin port, and the people of the city, learn the correct time.

From safer navigation came bigger ships, larger cargoes and heavier loads, requiring deeper water and more berths. The innovative engineers of the Port and Docks Board rose to the challenge, embarking on one of the most significant infrastructural developments in modern Irish history.

The advent of containerisation, where goods are carried in sealed metal containers, changed trade and shipping everywhere. From the second part of the twentieth century, only those ports that had the dynamism to expand and the space and water depth to accommodate large container ships could survive. Dublin port met and surmounted the challenges. New quays, gantries, container parks and deeper berths have replaced the cranes, nets, warehouses and manual labour that had handled cargo for centuries.

In today's shipping, transporting cargo is enabled through the use of atomic clocks, computers and container gantries directed by satellites in medium-earth orbit.

As the port has expanded eastward, its links to the city and its people have weakened. The docks became a specialised industrial area out of sight of most of the city's population. Plans are afoot now, as part of wider infrastructural developments, that will bring the citizens of the city back into the heart of their port, for recreation, cultural activities and contact with nature.

Ian Elliott documented all these innovations, in the port, in astronomy, timekeeping and science, and turned them into a fascinating story. His deep knowledge of so many areas of science and maritime affairs was matched by a clear, authoritative and accessible writing style.

Sadly, although he put the story of Dublin Port down on paper, he did not live to see it published. He died in 2015.

It became my privilege as editor to prepare his manuscript for publication. This mainly involved bringing the narrative up to the present and explaining some scientific terms to the non-specialist. It is Ian Elliott's voice, through his clear prose, that you will hear in your mind as you read the story. If his book re-introduces Dublin's citizens to their port and its everyday importance for the city and country, and gives a deeper appreciation of the wonders of Dublin Bay – the only UNESCO Biosphere that contains, within it, a capital city – I am sure Ian Elliott would be well pleased with the results of his labours.

Peigín Doyle

1. Dublin Port and its engineers

I must go down to the seas again, to the lonely sea and the sky,
And all I ask is a tall ship and a star to steer her by;
And the wheel's kick and the wind's song and the white sail's shaking,
And a grey mist on the sea's face, and a grey dawn breaking.
Sea Fever by John Masefield (1878–1967)

1.1 The Settlement of Dublin

The area around Dublin Bay and the river Liffey, on the east coast of Ireland, has been settled since at least the Middle Stone Age. In the late Iron Age, one of the five principal early roads, the *Slighe Cualann*, came from the south and crossed the river Liffey here on its way to the ritual capital at Tara. In time, the natural ford was augmented by a bridge probably made of lengths of timber laid over stakes or hurdles driven into the river bed. This gave Dublin its name in Irish, *Baile Átha Cliath*, the town of the ford of hurdles. An Early Christian settlement located near this ford later merged with a ninth century Viking trading post to become the Scandinavian city of *Dubhlinn*, meaning the Dark Pool. It developed into a national administrative centre under the later Anglo-Norman invaders and became the modern capital of Ireland.

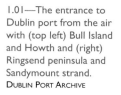

1.01—The entrance to Dublin port from the air with (top left) Bull Island and Howth and (right) Ringsend peninsula and Sandymount strand.
DUBLIN PORT ARCHIVE

The story of Dublin is most often told as the evolution from river ford to national capital but the development of Dublin could not have occurred without its port whose trade drove the city's prosperity for a thousand years. Though city and port are intricately linked, this book recounts the history of Dublin port.

1.2 Dublin Port

There is no better way to arrive in Dublin than by sea. Coming from the east, the first indication that we are nearing the port is the Kish Lighthouse warning seafarers away from the Kish sandbank, which lies about 11 km from the coast. Over the years, the Kish Bank has been a notorious hazard and 55 wrecks are listed for the area. The worst single incident was the loss of the mailboat, the RMS *Leinster*, which was torpedoed by a German submarine on 10 October 1918. She sank six kilometres east of the Kish with the loss of over 500 lives, the greatest single loss of life in the Irish Sea.

Soon the great panorama of Dublin Bay comes in sight, stretching from the Wicklow Mountains in the south to the Howth peninsula in the north. It is easy to pick out the Sugarloaf Mountain, Bray Head, Dalkey Island and Dun Laoghaire harbour with its lighthouse. The mouth of the bay is about 10 km wide between Dun Laoghaire lighthouse on the south side and the Baily lighthouse on the north side. Next, the twin chimney stacks of the Pidgeon House power station appear and then the outstretched arms of the North and South Bull Walls with their lighthouses. The North Bull Island in the northerly part of the bay features the five kilometre-long sandy beach of Dollymount Strand and reminds us that Dublin Bay has been fashioned by civil engineers over the past couple of centuries to better serve the needs of those who use the port. This chapter tells how these changes were achieved.

It is not known for certain when the city of Dublin was founded but there is evidence that the region was inhabited by hunter-gatherers during the Middle Stone Age, around 8000 BC. Dublin Bay and the river Liffey offered a convenient gateway to the central plain of Ireland. The original settlement was located on the southern bank of the Liffey at *Áth Cliath*, a monastic compound near to Ussher's Island. The ford was an important crossing-place for at least four trade routes.

In AD 795, the Vikings raided the monastery on Lambay Island and by 841 they had a permanent camp at the mouth of the Liffey from which they were expelled by the Irish in 902. The Vikings returned to Dublin in 917 as traders and they established a settlement on high ground on the south bank of the Liffey at *Dubhlinn* on the river Poddle where they moored their boats. In the tenth and eleventh centuries, Dublin became an important trading centre dealing in luxury goods as well as everyday commodities. By the twelfth century, it had a fleet of over 200 ships that traded not only with English ports but also with the Continent.

With the coming of the Anglo-Normans at the end of the twelfth century, there was an influx of settlers from south-west England and south Wales who were employed in a great building programme. Churches and public buildings were built or rebuilt in stone, which came by sea from quarries in Ireland, England and Wales. The existing timber jetties became inadequate and were replaced by a succession of new structures reaching further and further into the river. Eventually, in the early fourteenth century, a stone quay wall was built along the line of present-day Wood Quay. However, despite provision of these quays, Dalkey Sound was the main anchorage for large ships from abroad. Their cargoes were transferred into lighters with draughts shallow enough to enable them to sail up the Liffey.

In 1583, the City Assembly repaired and rebuilt the bridge described as the 'old bridge' near the ford of the hurdles. It had been erected in 1210 to replace a bridge dating back to Viking times that had been replaced several times. The present bridge joining High Street on the south bank to Church Street on the north bank was completed in 1818 and named 'Whitworth Bridge' after the Lord Lieutenant of the time. In 1938 it was renamed 'Father Mathew Bridge' to mark the centenary of the Father Mathew temperance movement. In 1697, Parliament Street was connected to Capel Street by the building of Essex Bridge, later rebuilt as Grattan Bridge. A new Custom House was built on Wellington Quay in 1707 and it appears in the picture by Joseph Tudor dated 1753 (see p. 4).

Under Anglo-Norman law, control of tidal waters was vested in the Crown. As a result of increasing trade in the sixteenth century, responsibility for the upkeep of quays and slips was transferred to individual citizens. In return for maintaining the quays and slips they were entitled to levy a charge on ships using the quays and slips. However, over the years refuse was dumped in the river and old hulks were allowed to rot in the river and the estuary. In 1593, the City Council had to order the removal of all hulks under penalty of imprisonment.

Dublin Bay was shallow and posed many hazards for mariners. Originally the bay had two large sand banks, the North Bull and the South Bull, either side of the mouth of the Liffey, which were

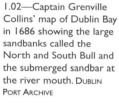

1.02—Captain Grenville Collins' map of Dublin Bay in 1686 showing the large sandbanks called the North and South Bull and the submerged sandbar at the river mouth. DUBLIN PORT ARCHIVE

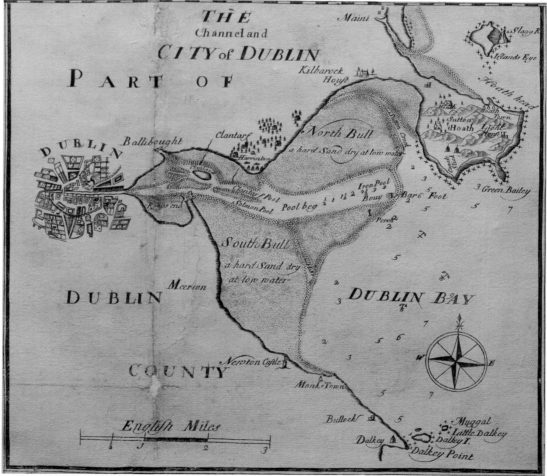

exposed at low water. In addition, a shallow submerged sandbar at a depth of six feet at low water connected the North and South Bulls and limited access to the river. The municipal archives contain a description of the estuary:

> The tides uninterruptedly expanded themselves over vast tracts of north and south strands . . . and in their progress towards the city branched out into many channels, both curved and intricate.

Ships moored in the bay awaiting high water were exposed to easterly winds, which often drove them onto the hard strands of the Bulls. Clontarf and Ringsend offered some shelter for unloading vessels but many ships and their crews were lost on the treacherous coastline from Howth to Dalkey.

In 1686, Charles II commissioned Captain Grenville Collins to survey the harbours of Britain and Ireland. His map of Dublin Bay shows the great extent of the North and South Bulls and the narrow channel leading up river. Ringsend, situated on a long, narrow peninsula separated from the rest of Dublin by the estuary of the river Dodder, was a convenient landing place for large ships. It was at Ringsend that the British Parliamentary general, Oliver Cromwell, landed with 13,000 troops in August 1649.

1.3 The Ballast Office

After several attempts at reform, an act was passed in 1707 entitled 'An Act for Cleansing the Port, Harbour and River of Dublin and for Erecting a Ballast Office in the said City'; this came to be known as 'The Ballast Office Act'. Power to carry out the necessary work was vested in the Corporation. The act provided that 'The Lord Mayor, Sheriffs, commons and citizens of the city of Dublin . . . are hereby constituted and ordained keepers and conservators of the Port of Dublin'.

The General Assembly of the Corporation set up a committee to manage the business of the

1.03—Ships moored beside the first Customs House built beside Essex Bridge in 1707. ROYAL MUSEUMS GREENWICH

Ballast Office and premises were acquired in Essex Street. One of the first actions of the Ballast Office Committee was to order three lighters for raising ballast from the river bed and supplying it to ships for a charge. It was important for the stability of ships that, after unloading, the cargo was replaced with sufficient ballast to make them seaworthy. When not employed in raising ballast, the lighters were used to create a new shipping channel above Ringsend.

In 1713, the Assembly granted an estate on the city side of Ringsend to Sir John Rogerson who immediately began to enclose his new land with a massive sea wall now known as the South Wall. Meanwhile, the Ballast Office had been stabilising the northern bank of the river by laying down kishes (baskets filled with stones) and backing them with sand and gravel. By October 1712, 686 kishes were in place along the line of present-day Eden Quay and Custom House Quay.

1.4 The Great South Wall

In April 1715, the Assembly approved the building of an embankment to prevent the encroachment of sand from the South Bull into the shipping channel. The embankment ran eastwards from Ringsend. It was made by driving oak piles into the boulder clay of the bay and anchoring them with kishes and woven wattles. The embankment, known as 'The Piles', was completed in 1731 but proved inadequate to retain the sand of the South Bull.

In the mid-1740s, the Ballast Committee decided to build a double-walled stone embankment from Ringsend along the line of the old piles to the 'Green Patch', an area near the present Pigeon House Harbour. The embankment was constructed by building two parallel granite walls, filling the intervening space with stones and rubble and covering the infill with a layer of granite blocks. The blocks, each weighing up to one ton, were quarried from the hills behind Dalkey and Dun Laoghaire and transported across the bay in barges. Bullock Harbour, Coliemore Harbour and Sandycove Harbour were constructed to enable the loading of the blocks onto the barges. The granite blocks

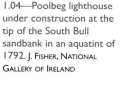

1.04—Poolbeg lighthouse under construction at the tip of the South Bull sandbank in an aquatint of 1792. J. FISHER, NATIONAL GALLERY OF IRELAND

were designed to interlock and needed no bonding material. This section of 8,000 feet was completed in 1756.

Construction of the second section of wall began in 1761 with laying the foundation of the Poolbeg Lighthouse at the very tip of the South Bull sandbank and working back to the shore. This section of 10,500 feet joined the first section at Pidgeon House Harbour and the Great South Wall was completed in 1795. With a total length of 3.5 miles (5.6 km), it was the world's longest sea-wall at the time of its construction and it remains one of the longest in Europe.

On the evening of 29 September 1767, Rogerson's Quay was crowded with people to see the first light from the new Poolbeg Lighthouse, the first to be lit with candles instead of a coal-fired beacon. The new lighthouse had an octagonal lantern with eight heavy glass windows. A stone staircase with an iron balustrade led to the second storey, where an iron gallery surrounded the whole building. The candles were replaced by oil lamps in 1786. In 1818 the gallery was removed and the tower was raised to its present height of 63 feet.

1.05—The Stena Line ferry *Ocean Majesty* passes the Poolbeg lighthouse which still marks the entrance to Dublin port today. DENIS BERGIN, DUBLIN PORT ARCHIVE, 2014

1.5 The Pidgeon House

About 1760, the Ballast Office constructed a timber blockhouse on the Green Patch and hired a John Pidgeon as watchman. Pidgeon and his family were allowed to reside in the blockhouse, which was a substantial building. Pidgeon was permitted to sell refreshments to the passengers arriving or departing on the packet ships. The work on the port, including the lighthouse, were of great interest to the citizens of Dublin and Pidgeon and other boatmen were kept busy at weekends ferrying sightseers from Ringsend down river. Pidgeon and his family prospered until August 1786 when they were attacked by a gang of four men. Unfortunately, Pidgeon and his son died of their injuries but his daughters survived and eventually had good fortune. The story of Pidgeon and his family appeared in the *Dublin Penny Journal* in 1833 and is reproduced in Appendix 1. Pidgeon's name (now

Pigeon) lives on in the names of places in the vicinity.

In 1787, the Ballast Board appointed an inspector of works, Francis Tunstall, a stonecutter and mason. In 1791, the board constructed a small tidal harbour at the Pidgeon House, which became known as Pidgeon House Harbour, and Tunstall was put in charge of the area. The purpose of the harbour was to avoid the need to ferry passengers to packet ships anchored in the river channel. The fact that the harbour dried out at low water led to delays and to the eventual transfer of the packet station to a new harbour at Howth in 1818.

By 1793, the need for more accommodation for travellers led to the construction of the Pidgeon House Hotel and Mrs Tunstall was employed as manageress. From 1794 onwards Tunstall supervised the building of the quay walls and parapets from Aston Quay westwards.

The 1798 Rising and the threat of a French invasion caused the government to request the temporary use of the 'quays, buildings and adjoining land at the blockhouse for military defence purposes'. The board resisted but the Pidgeon House Fort was constructed and after a lot of negotiation the premises were transferred in 1814 for £100,183.

1.06—Pidgeon House harbour in the 18th century. NATIONAL GALLERY OF IRELAND

1.6 Improving Dublin

Meanwhile, since 1757 the Wide Streets Commission under its Chief Commissioner, John Beresford, was transforming the old medieval city by demolishing or widening old streets or by creating entirely new ones such as Sackville Street (now O'Connell Street). Thus, the main north–south axis of the city was moved eastwards from Capel Street and Parliament Street.

Beresford was also the prime mover in the campaign to build a new Custom House. Many merchants who had property in the older parts of the city were opposed to the spread of the city eastwards and, when the foundation trenches were opened in 1781, they organised a mob of several thousand in protest. The original architect was Thomas Cooley, who died in March 1784. Nevertheless, building went ahead under the supervision of another architect, James Gandon (1743–1823), and was completed in November 1791 at a cost of £200,000, a huge sum at the time. This was Gandon's first major commission. He next designed Carlisle Bridge to join Sackville Street to

1.07—The Custom House, which replaced the old building upriver at Essex bridge in 1791.
DUBLIN PORT ARCHIVE

the south side of the river. It was an elegant structure with three semi-circular arches in granite with a Portland stone balustrade and was completed in 1794.

Around 1782, the Irish House of Commons became dissatisfied with the financial affairs of the Ballast Office. There was concern about the continual requests for money to complete the South Wall and about the way the grants were managed. The Dublin city merchants led by John Beresford promoted a bill to replace the Ballast Committee with a new 'body corporate and politick', independent of Dublin Corporation, called the Corporation for Preserving and Improving the Port of Dublin (generally known as the Ballast Board). The act came into force on 8 May 1786 and the new board lost no time in bringing in reforms.

One of the consequences of the increase of activity was the need for larger offices for the Ballast Board. After renting temporary premises in Sackville Street for three years, the board acquired a site at 21 Westmoreland Street in 1801 under a lease of 175 years. Following the death of Francis Tunstall in 1800, the board appointed George Halpin as the new Inspector of Works. Halpin was a builder

1.08 — Dublin's elegant
streets seen from Carlisle
Bridge with the new
Ballast Office building
acquired in 1801 on the
right. NATIONAL LIBRARY OF
IRELAND

by trade with no engineering qualifications but through his attention to detail he made a considerable contribution to the development of the port. In 1830 Halpin's son, George Halpin jun., a qualified civil engineer, was appointed assistant to his father.

One initiative of the new board was the formation of a lifeboat service with three boats stationed at Clontarf, Sandycove and Sutton and, later, two at Howth and the Pidgeon House. Eventually only three were retained – Kingstown, Howth and the Pidgeon House (Poolbeg). In 1824, the National Institution for the Preservation of Life from Shipwreck was established and in 1854 the name was changed to the Royal National Lifeboat Institution.

1.7 Capt. Bligh's Survey of Dublin Bay

In 1800, Capt. William Bligh (1754–1817) was commissioned to carry out a survey of Dublin Bay. Aged 46, for Bligh this commission was a placid interval in a very turbulent career. Only 11 years previously, Bligh and 18 loyal crewmen had survived a 47-day voyage in an open boat after the mutiny of his ship, the *Bounty*.

Bligh carried out a detailed survey of the bay, paying special attention to the flow of the tides. His main recommendation was for a wall running eastwards from the junction of the North Wall and the East Wall and parallel to the Great South Wall. It was marked by a line on his survey chart ending on the most easterly tip of the North Bull sandbank. The wall had two purposes: to carry river sediment out to sea and to prevent the incursion of sand into the shipping channel. Bligh's proposal was recommended to the Lord Lieutenant but the matter was deferred to consider a proposal by George Maquay and Leland Crosthwaite. Their suggestion was to build a pier running in a south-easterly direction from Clontarf to a proposed new lighthouse sited opposite to the Poolbeg lighthouse. The new pier would impound a great volume of water which, on the ebb, would scour the seabed and deepen the entrance channel.

In 1802, the respected Scottish civil engineer John Rennie (1761–1821) was asked for his opinion on the proposals and he wrote: 'The improvement of Dublin Harbour is perhaps one of the most difficult subjects which has ever come under the consideration of the civil engineer'. Rennie supported the North Wall proposal and even suggested a tidal reservoir on the South Wall, which would fill and empty through an opening in the South Wall.

1.8 The Great North Wall

The sale of the Pidgeon House premises in 1814 allowed the Ballast Board to put aside funds for the future development of the port. Although the Great North Wall project was considered several times, no progress was made until 1818 when a new survey of the outer harbour was carried out by Halpin and Francis Giles, a hydrographer in the Admiralty. The first action was the construction of a wooden bridge over the channel between the North Bull sandbank and Clontarf; this was completed in April 1821. Construction on the wall itself started in November 1821 and was completed by 1824 at a cost of £95,000. Most of the wall stands clear of flood tides and has a paved surface but the last stage is in the form of a breakwater, submerged at high tide. The total length of the Wall is 2.9 km and it terminates in the North Bull Lighthouse.

The building of the North Wall achieved its objectives and the depth of water at the harbour entrance increased from 1.8 metres to 4.8 metres over the first half century. In addition, the sand that accumulated on the seaward side gradually grew into what is known now as the Bull Island stretching five kilometres towards Howth and about 800 metres in width. Dubliners were quick to appreciate the new amenity and soon it was a popular place for swimming and walking. In 1889, the Royal Dublin Golf Club, then located in the Phoenix Park, sought and received permission to lay out a golf course at the city end of the island, and to construct a clubhouse. During World War I, the British army commandeered the whole island for training purposes and used the golf clubhouse for officers' quarters. In 1921 a second golf club, St Anne's, was established.

1.9 Howth Harbour

In 1807, the government decided to build a harbour at Howth to replace the inadequate facilities at Pidgeon House Harbour. Capt. George Taylor prepared the plan and supervised the early stages of construction. On his resignation in 1808, he was replaced by John Aird under the direction of John Rennie. There was much debate over the choice of site for the new pier (the present east pier) and many thought tidal currents would lead to silting. Rennie suggested a second (west) pier and it was completed in 1813. The harbour opened to mail packets in 1818 but the advent of steamship packets soon brought complaints about the level of rock in the harbour and silting at the entrance. On completion, Howth harbour was vested in the Ballast Board.

1.10 Kingstown Harbour

In November 1807, one of the greatest marine tragedies in Dublin Bay took place when the packet ship *Prince of Wales* and the troop transport *Rochdale*, sailing from Pidgeon House Harbour, were wrecked in a storm on the rocks between Dun Laoghaire and Blackrock. The *Prince of Wales* was wrecked near where Blackrock Park is now and the *Rochdale* hit the shore at Seapoint. Three hundred and eighty people were drowned, many of them soldiers and their families. The calamity caused a public outcry and a demand for a harbour of refuge on the south side of Dublin Bay.

John Rennie drew up plans for a single (east) pier at Dun Laoghaire and work started in 1816, the granite being taken from Dalkey quarry. In order to give shelter from north-west gales and to prevent silting, a second pier was built, the present west pier. At the conclusion of the state visit of George IV in 1821, his departure from the new harbour was marked by the re-naming of the town and its harbour to 'Kingstown'. John Rennie died in 1821 but his son, also called John, continued to supervise the work. After a timber jetty was built at the east pier, the Post Office transferred the packet steamers from Howth to Kingstown in January 1834. The completion of the railway between Kingstown and Dublin in 1834 also assisted the movement of mails. In 1836, Dun Laoghaire and Kingstown harbours were vested in a new body, Kingstown Harbour Commissioners, and became an enclave within the port of Dublin. The East Pier and its lighthouse were completed in 1842 and the West Pier and its lighthouse six years later. The new harbour was 102 hectares in area, making it the largest artificial harbour in the world at that time. The bay formed between the harbour and The Forty Foot is still known as Scotsman's Bay after Rennie.

1.11 Lighthouses

In 1810, an act of Parliament transferred responsibility for the 14 lighthouses round the coast of Ireland from the Revenue Commissioners to the Ballast Board. The first priority was to improve navigational aids for the packet ships entering and leaving Dublin port. A lightship was placed on the Kish sandbank and came into operation in November 1811. A new lighthouse designed by George Halpin was built on the Baily promontory on Howth. It replaced lighthouses that had been established at the 'summit' near the present car park. The original lighthouse, built about 1667, consisted of a small cottage and an adjoining square tower, which supported a coal-fired beacon. It was replaced in 1790 by a circular tower about six metres high, displaying an oil light. However, due to its height above sea level, the light was frequently obscured by cloud and was quite ineffective. The new lighthouse with accommodation for the keeper was completed in March 1814.

Between 1810 and 1867, the number of Irish lighthouses increased from 14 to 72 under the direction of the Halpins. George Halpin established 53 new lighthouses in addition to modernising 15 others. He established the Irish lighthouse service's administration and managerial procedures as well as continuing to oversee the development of Dublin port.

1.12 Growth of Trade

By the middle of the nineteenth century there was a dramatic increase in trade through the port. A total movement of vessels of about 400,000 tons in 1836 rose to almost 1.4 million tons in 1866. Moreover, whereas ships of 400 tons were regarded as large in the 1830s, deep sea vessels of 1,000 tons were common in 1866. The shipping companies demanded deeper water at the quays to enable vessels to remain afloat at low water. The board decided to build timber wharves along the North and South Walls and a basin was dredged at the end of the North Wall to a depth of 16 feet at low water; the basin became known as 'Halpin's pond'. Halpin introduced a steam dredger in 1814 and it was replaced by two more powerful dredgers in 1930.

Halpin senior died in July 1854 while on one of his lighthouse inspections. His son, also named George, was appointed in his place with Thomas Ramsey, an engineer, as his assistant. Ramsey resigned in 1856 and the board appointed Bindon Blood Stoney (1828–1909) Assistant Engineer. Stoney had a Diploma in Civil Engineering from Trinity College and had spent two years as observing assistant to William Parsons, 3rd Earl of Rosse, at Birr Castle before a brief spell of surveying

1.09—Ships moored at Eden Quay and Georges Quay in 1843 in the earliest photograph of Dublin port by Revd Calvert Jones. ROYAL MUSEUMS GREENWICH

work for the Aranjuez to Almansa railway in Spain. In 1854, he was appointed resident engineer on the Boyne Viaduct under James Barton, the chief engineer of the railway. The bridge was constructed from large wrought-iron lattice girders on the suggestion of Sir John Macneill. Stoney successfully applied a theory of stresses in continuous girders that had been developed by his uncle Professor William Bindon Blood of Queen's College, Galway. He later published *The Theory of Strains in Girders and Similar Structures,* which was to become a classic text. The total length of the bridge was 1760 feet (538 metres) making it the longest span in the world at the time of its completion in 1875.

As Halpin junior had to devote most of his time to lighthouse work, involving long absences from Dublin, Stoney was in practice acting port engineer. Stoney's first task was to supervise the completion

1.10—Bindon Blood Stoney, one of the great engineers who built Dublin port. DUBLIN PORT ARCHIVE

of a new graving dock at East Wall that had been designed by Halpin junior. The graving dock was needed to carry out repairs to ships and it was made 400 feet long by 80 feet wide to take the latest mail steamers. The dock was built by William Dargan (1799–1867), the eminent railway contractor, and from its start in 1853 took seven years to complete. It was described as '… one of the most excellent specimens of material and workmanship…'. In 1859, Stoney was made Executive Engineer and given authority to sign accounts.

1.13 Stoney in Charge

With an increased need for dredging, the continued disposal of spoil on Sandymount Strand became unacceptable to the residents of the Sandymount and Merrion districts. Stoney proposed the purchase of barges of 1000-ton capacity with bottom-opening doors. The barges were loaded with spoil and towed to deep water beyond the Baily lighthouse where it was dumped and dispersed by tidal currents.

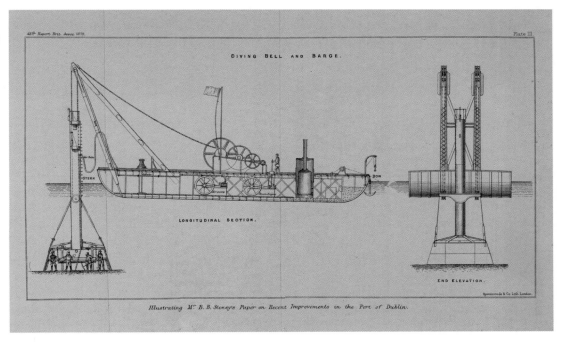

1.11—Bindon Blood Stoney's design for the barge and diving bell used to build an extension to the North Wall. DUBLIN PORT ARCHIVE

In January 1861, Stoney proposed a plan for the long-term improvement of the port. He suggested the continuation of the North Wall eastwards beyond the junction with the East Wall and the construction of a basin that would provide deepwater berths for shipping. Instead of using the traditional method of a piled cofferdam, Stoney proposed making large concrete blocks each weighing 350 tons. The foundation for the blocks would be excavated by a dredger with the final levelling carried out manually by men working in a diving bell. The bell was made of iron and consisted of a chamber 20 feet square with a shaft and airlock for access. Stoney maintained that his method would be considerably cheaper than traditional methods. When Stoney submitted his report, Halpin junior was away from Dublin on lighthouse duties and was piqued that he was not consulted beforehand. Halpin defended the traditional methods but in the end Stoney's arguments were

1.12—Workers preparing for underwater on the port. DUBLIN PORT ARCHIVE

accepted. Halpin, with his health failing, decided to retire in March 1862 and Stoney was appointed Engineer.

In 1864, the board decided to proceed with the North Wall Extension and Stoney was instructed to obtain tenders for the shear float and the diving bell that he had designed. The shear float was constructed by Harland and Wolff of Belfast. Grendon and Company of Drogheda built the diving bell and its pontoon. The equipment was delivered in 1866 but the project was put on hold as the reconstitution of the port authority was under consideration.

As a result of agitation from traders and shipowners, the composition of the board was changed by the 'Dublin Port and Docks Board' Act of 1867 to give them representation. In addition, the act severed the lighthouse and port functions of the board, giving the title 'Commissioners of Irish Lights' to the lighthouse authority and 'Dublin Port and Docks Board' to the port authority. Also in 1867, the engineer's office was moved from the Ballast Office to the North Wall. From 1868, Stoney was Engineer in Chief of the port and remained in that post for just over 30 years.

Work on the extension to the North Wall Quay commenced in 1869. A new wharf was built east of the graving dock for the construction of the 350-ton concrete blocks. The procedure for lifting the blocks involved the shear float moving bow-first up to the platform of the wharf, which was set low near the water. After the crane was attached, the ballast tanks in the after end of the shear float were filled and this tilted the barge enough to lift the block. The barge was then towed to the laying position. The shear float was described as 'A powerful tubular girder…which distributed the shearing strains over the whole area…'. The first block was laid on 27 May 1871 and work continued at a steady pace. Also in 1871, John Purser Griffith was appointed Stoney's assistant.

By 1882, over 2000 feet of quay with a depth of 22 feet had been built on the river side of the works and over 1600 feet to a depth of 24 feet on the basin side. The Prince and Princess of Wales visited Dublin in 1885 and on 11 April they inspected the new extension and the Princess formally

1.13—The Diving Bell at night. CONOR McCABE, 2020

opened the 70-acre Alexandra Basin. At the time it was widely rumoured that Stoney would be knighted but nothing came of it.

1.14 Marriage and Honours for Stoney

Meanwhile, in 1879, aged 51, Stoney married Susannah Frances, daughter of Francis Walker of Grangemore, Raheny, Co. Dublin (subsequently the residence of former Taoiseach Charles J. Haughey). In 1881, he moved with his wife and new-born son, George Bindon, from Wellington Road to a substantial terraced house and mews at 14 Elgin Road. The couple had also three daughters, Priscilla, Anne and Laura. Shortly after his marriage, Stoney was awarded an Honorary Doctor of Laws by Dublin University and was also elected a Fellow of the Royal Society. He was also a member of the Royal Irish Academy and served as President of the Institution of Civil Engineers in Ireland.

In 1872, Stoney began to advise the 4th Earl of Rosse on the rebuilding of the 36-inch telescope, which the 3rd Earl had constructed 30 years earlier. The original telescope had a wooden alt-azimuth mounting that was not suitable for photography. Stoney designed an equatorial metal mounting that was much more convenient for the observer. George Strype of Grendon's in Drogheda was employed as mechanical engineering consultant of the project.

1.15 Stoney the Bridge Builder

Stoney was involved in the design and construction of three bridges over the Liffey. The first of these projects was the rebuilding of Essex Bridge, which linked Capel Street to Parliament Street. Its narrowness and steep approaches contributed to traffic congestion. Stoney worked with Parke Neville, the City Engineer, to produce a design that replaced the original semi-circular arches by elliptical ones and the footpaths were carried beyond the faces of the arches on cantilevered iron girders. The work started in 1873 and was completed in 1874. After rebuilding and widening, the bridge was named Grattan Bridge after Henry Grattan (1746–1820). The completed bridge was severely criticised for not being as elegant as the other Liffey bridges but Stoney would have been well aware of the need to produce an economical solution.

The second project was the replacement of Carlisle Bridge, which had been erected in 1761 to the design of James Gandon. The bridge was only 40 feet wide and was hump-backed. In 1860, a survey showed that, between 9 a.m. and 7 p.m. on an average working day, some 10,000 vehicles crossed the bridge. The Corporation set up a committee in 1861 to report on the practicality and cost of rebuilding. The committee recommended that the new bridge should be as level as possible and be the same width as Sackville Street.

1.14—The 1761 Carlisle Bridge built by James Gandon was replaced to Stoney's design in 1880. It was renamed O'Connell Bridge. DUBLIN PORT ARCHIVE

In 1864, it was decided to hold a competition for the best design and some 40 entries were received. The committee selected three designs but none was ideal and attempts to get the Westminster Parliament to vote the necessary funds were not successful. Negotiations dragged on for 12 more years until 1876 when the board agreed to promote a Bill in Parliament and the Dublin Port and Docks Board (Bridges) Act, 1876, received Royal Assent on 27 June 1876. The Act enabled the board to rebuild Carlisle Bridge and to construct a new swivel bridge to the east. Both bridges were designed by Stoney and work began in May 1877.

Stoney's design for the new Carlisle Bridge consisted of three elliptical arches. The scheme was

to build the new arches alongside the old bridge and to use the thoroughfare over them to carry traffic while the old bridge was being demolished and rebuilt.

When completed, the board named the new bridge Carlisle Bridge and a handsome red marble tablet carried the name on the eastern side of the bridge. However, the Corporation had other ideas and named the bridge after Daniel O'Connell (1775–1847) as they were in the process of erecting a statue to him at the south end of Sackville Street. They placed a bronze-green plate over the marble tablet and O'Connell Bridge was finally opened to the public on 6 August 1880.

1.16 Father Pat Noise

A rather different sort of plaque appeared on the parapet on the western side of the bridge in 2004 with the inscription:

> This plaque commemorates
> Fr. Pat Noise
> Advisor to Peadar Clancey
> He died under suspicious
> circumstances when his
> carriage plunged into the
> Liffey on August 10th 1919.
> Erected by the HSTI

The plaque was put into position by a couple of pranksters who owned up when the matter was brought to the attention of Dublin City Council in 2006. They claimed that the plaque was a tribute to their father and that 'Fr. Pat Noise' was a play of words on *pater noster*, Latin for 'our father'. Peadar Clancy (misspelt on the plaque) was an actual IRA officer killed on the evening of Bloody Sunday in November 1920.

The plaque was fitted into a depression on the parapet left by the removal of the control box for the ill-fated 'Millennium Countdown' clock installed in the waters of the Liffey in March 1996. As the underwater digital clock was very unreliable, it and the control box were removed in December 1996. The City Council threatened to remove the unauthorised plaque but a sub-committee recommended its retention. The plaque was removed in March 2007 during restoration work on the bridge but a second plaque was installed, again surreptitiously. Removal was once more threatened but was stopped by Councillor Dermot Lacey who insisted that the Council's order should stand.

1.16—O'Connell Bridge today, viewed from the east. MARTA LOPEZ ALARCÓN

1.17 The Swing Bridge at Beresford Place

The swing bridge connecting Tara Street to Beresford Place was constructed at the same time as O'Connell Bridge. It consisted of two approach spans each of 37 feet and a central swing span of 127 feet, giving two 40-foot openings for navigation. The ironwork and the machinery were supplied by Skerne Ironworks of Darlington. The swing bridge was opened on 26 August 1879 and named Butt Bridge at the request of the Corporation. Purser Griffith deputised for Stoney who, it seems, was on his honeymoon. The bridge operated for barely eight years before the construction of the Liffey Viaduct (Loopline) blocked all river traffic except for the Guinness barges and small craft. As early as 1886, proposals were made to the board for the widening of the bridge but it was not until 1932 that the central swing span was removed and replaced with a single reinforced concrete arch to form the present-day Butt Bridge.

1.17—The central section of the new swing bridge connecting Tara Street and Beresford Place under construction. It was named Butt Bridge. DUBLIN PORT ARCHIVE

1.18 Bindon Stoney: Retirement and Death

In 1897, Stoney suffered some ill-health arising from a severe chill. He had a recurrence of a bronchial condition and tendered his resignation in December 1898. After more than 42 years' service to Dublin port, Stoney relinquished his post to his faithful assistant John Purser Griffith. There is no doubt that Stoney's service to the port was valued by the board and by his colleagues. The staff and workmen spoke of their appreciation in the following terms:

The Port of Dublin must ever remain a monument of your genius and engineering skill. ... The great strength and durability of the works attests to the soundness of his ideas and his positive genius for initiative in his profession.

Stoney enjoyed a decade of retirement but on 23 January 1909 he learnt by telegram from Australia that his son, George Bindon, had died the previous day, apparently from tuberculosis. George Bindon's early death at 27 was a great blow to Stoney and caused him to go into a rapid decline. He died at his residence at 14 Elgin Road, Dublin, on 5 May 1909. Many tributes were paid to Stoney. Perhaps the address given at his funeral by the Revd Robert Walsh, D.D., captures best his personality:

If rare intellectual attainments and great worth of character deserve special honour and special notice, the late Dr Stoney is entitled to these, for he held a chief place among those of his contempories [sic] who most deserve honour and respect. ...

He was not merely a distinguished engineer, one of the chiefs of a great profession; he was a man of wide culture, of varied reading, of remarkable information. He was endowed with intellectual gifts of no common order. These, united to genuine goodness and kindliness of heart, made him a

1.18—Stoney's swing bridge in place with channels for river traffic on either side of the central span and the new loopline railway bridge overhead. DUBLIN PORT ARCHIVE

delightful friend and companion. He had the happy gift of making you feel at ease with him, when discussing subjects on which he knew more than you. Distinguished by a marked independence of character, possessed of a store of information, his unassuming nature never unduly asserted itself. Any trace of pride of intellect was entirely absent from him; to know him was to love him; to know him well was to love and honour him the more. For deeper in him than his culture was that which gave his friendship its real charm, this was his absolute sincerity and simplicity of character, a more guileless man I never came in contact with. It is too often the inveterate tendency of very clever men to use their great gifts with the object of influencing others for their own purposes. Through the long years I have known our friend, the thing that impressed me as marked feature of his character was the love of truth, for its own sake, and his ceaseless desire to attain it and promote it because it was the right. He was above all petty aims or devious methods; he was essentially an honest man. In working with him you noticed he always formed an independent judgement on each subject under consideration. If he thought it his duty to take a different view from yours you felt so assured of the sincerity of his motive, that whether with you or against you in counsel, you were glad to have him as a colleague.

There is no doubt that Bindon Blood Stoney was a very remarkable man. But there were many other remarkable Stoneys and their achievements are recounted in Appendix 5.

1.19 Griffith at the Helm

John Purser Griffith (1848–1938) was well qualified to assume the post of Engineer in Chief after 27 years as Stoney's assistant. He was born on 5 October 1848 at Holyhead where his father was Congregational minister. Griffith owed his second name to a longstanding friendship between his father and John Tertius Purser, owner of Rathmines Castle, whose great-grandfather John (Primus)

1.19—John Purser Griffith who succeeded Bindon Blood Stoney as port Engineer in Chief.

1.20—The 100-ton crane that served the port from 1905. DUBLIN PORT ARCHIVE

and father John (Secundus) both worked as senior brewers for Guinness in Dublin and became partners in the firm in 1820. Tertius Purser joined Guinness in 1830 and, by the time he had retired, had amassed a considerable fortune. Tertius' brother Edward Purser was the father of the artist Sarah Purser (1848–1943).

J.P. Griffith entered Trinity College and was awarded his Licence in Civil Engineering in 1868. He spent two years apprenticed to Bindon Stoney in Dublin port before going as assistant to the County Antrim Surveyor. In 1871, he returned to Dublin as assistant to Stoney and in the same year he married Tertius Purser's daughter, the wonderfully named Anna (Nina) Beniga Fridlezius Purser (1837–1912). The couple had two sons, John William and Frederick, and a daughter, Alice. Nina inherited Rathmines Castle when her brothers, both university professors and bachelors, predeceased her. When Nina died in 1912, Purser Griffith inherited the whole of her estate.

A large part of Purser Griffith's time was taken up with organising dredging activities in the port. In 1899, an Admiralty survey had shown deterioration in the depth of water on the bar and in the river channel. A Dutch firm was contracted to remove 750,000 tons of sand by suction dredger. In 1903, the board purchased a large suction dredger, named *Sandpiper*, to maintain the depth of water on the bar. In addition, almost 1000 feet of deepwater berthage was provided by extending the timber jetties at the North Wall. In 1905, a 100-ton crane was purchased from Germany and it remained a prominent port landmark until it was dismantled in 1987.

Purser Griffith served as President of the Institution of Civil Engineers of Ireland in 1887–89 and was a member of the Royal Commission on Canals and Waterways, 1906–1911. In the Coronation Honours of June 1911, he received a knighthood from George V for his valuable services to the Port and Docks Board and to the Royal Commission on Canals. He retired in 1913 and was succeeded by his son, John William Griffith (1875–1936).

Sir John remained a member of the Port and Docks Board but was critical and outspoken about its policy of reducing staff numbers to save money. In July 1916, he resigned from the board and the following day his son tendered his resignation as Engineer in Chief. He was succeeded by Joseph H. Mallagh.

Sir John set up in practice as a consulting engineer and his expertise was widely respected. He supported the reclamation of Irish bogs for agricultural use and was involved in the Leinster Carbonising Company, which aimed to develop power production from peat. He investigated the hydroelectric power potential of the river Liffey and drew up a scheme that eventually led to the creation of the Poulaphouca reservoir. He was awarded the Boyle Medal of the Royal Dublin Society (RDS) in 1931 and was granted the freedom of the city of Dublin in 1936. He died at Rathmines Castle on 21 October 1938.

1.20 Engineer in Chief Joseph H. Mallagh (1873–1959)

Joseph Mallagh studied engineering at Queen's College, Galway, where he graduated in 1896 with the degrees of BA and BE from the Royal University of Ireland. After graduation, he was employed on the improvement of waterworks in Downpatrick, Portadown, Banbridge and Boyle. He was engineer for Sligo harbour before his appointment as Chief Engineer to the Port and Docks Board in 1917.

Mallagh was concerned at the condition of the timber jetties at Alexandra Wharf used by Gouldings and the oil companies. He proposed replacing the jetties with a masonry quay. He designed

1.21—Butt Bridge today. The central span was replaced to form a continuous bridge in 1932.

caissons, which were essentially large reinforced concrete boxes, each 50 feet long by 30 feet wide, and were built in a slipway like a ship. Unlike Stoney's solid blocks, the caissons could float. They were built to the required height of 42 feet, towed into position and sunk on the site of the new quay. Then the caissons were filled with spoil from the dredgers and sealed. This construction took place between 1922 and 1931 and the new quay was named Alexandra Quay.

Mallagh's concept of floating caissons was recognised as a major advance in the field of port engineering. The principle was adopted in the construction of the Mulberry harbours that facilitated the rapid unloading of cargo during the Allied invasion of Normandy in 1944.

By the 1920s, Butt Bridge could not cope with the traffic using it. Mallagh designed a wider single-span bridge, which was completed in 1932. Mallagh retired in 1941 and was succeeded by Mr F.W. Bond.

1.21 Changes in Work and Administration

Great changes took place in Dublin port in the remainder of the twentieth century. Just as sail had given way to steam, so the stevedores and cranes gave way to containers and roll-on roll-off ships. These changes involved new work practices and great social upheaval for the workforce but were essential if the port were to maintain its commercial competitiveness.

1.22—Container shipping transformed how ports operate and cargo is handled. CONOR MCCABE PHOTOGRAPHY

23

1.23—The Port Centre building at Alexandra Road became the new headquarters of the Dublin Port Company in 1981. PETER MOLONEY PHOTOGRAPHY

Changes were also necessary in the administrative structure of the port. The Harbours Act 1946 implemented most of the recommendations of a tribunal that had reported in 1930. The act gave the Minister for Industry and Commerce general oversight over all harbour authorities in the state. The last meeting of the Port and Docks Board in the Ballast Office, Westmoreland Street, took place in February 1976. The board moved to temporary premises at Gandon House, Amiens Street. A new Port Centre was erected at Alexandra Road and all the board's administrative, clerical and technical staff were transferred to it in August 1981. The Port and Docks Board itself was wound up and Dublin Port Company was incorporated as a state-owned commercial company on 28 February 1997.

2. Time, clocks and navigation

2.1 Time and Navigation

The development of marine navigation, global shipping and modern ports has been bound up closely with the ability to accurately measure time, programme computers and build space satellites.

What is time? That question has occupied the minds of philosophers and scientists since time immemorial. As far as theoretical physicists are concerned, it is part of the great problem of reconciling the two major theories of the twentieth century – Relativity and Quantum Mechanics. For seafarers and navigators, knowing the time is essential for plotting where they are on the Earth's seas and how far they have travelled since their last position. Humanity has striven for millennia to measure time and seasons, devising ingenious and sometimes extremely sophisticated methods of measurement.

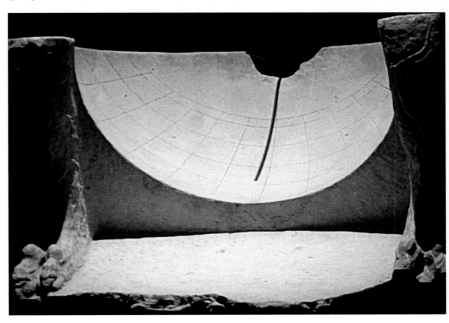

2.01—A Greek sundial based on the design of Berossus, the Babylonian priest who first described one.

2.2 The Longitude Problem

Finding an accurate way of establishing a ship's position at sea preoccupied thinkers and seafarers for centuries. In navigation, the process of calculating one's present position by using a previously known position, or fix, and using the direction and distance travelled is known as dead reckoning.

It is subject to cumulative errors and uncertain knowledge of cross winds and currents. In ancient times, the only way to measure a ship's speed was to throw a wooden log into the water and observe how fast it moved away from the ship. This method was called 'Heaving the Log' and was used until the sixteenth century when the 'Chip Log' method was invented.

The 'Chip Log' equipment consisted of a small, weighted wood panel that was attached to a reel of rope and a half-minute sandglass. The rope had knots every 50 feet along the reel. Sailors would throw the wooden panel into the sea from the stern of the ship and the rope would start unwinding from the reel. The faster the ship was moving, the faster the rope would unwind. By counting the number of knots that went overboard in half a minute, measured by the sandglass, they could tell the ship's speed. This is the origin of the knot measurement of speed at sea, a knot being one nautical mile per hour.

2.02—The 'Chip Log' equipment for measuring the speed of a ship at sea.
ROYAL MUSEUMS GREENWICH

Longitude is a measurement that marks one's position east or west of a given point on the Earth's surface. In mapping, imaginary lines drawn from north to south poles, called meridians, join places that are on the same longitude, which is usually expressed in degrees.

Time and longitude are closely connected in navigation. Local time, which can be estimated from the position of the Sun, varies significantly according to location because of the Sun's east to west movement across the sky. By comparing local time at the position where the Sun is observed to solar time at a fixed or agreed point, such as Greenwich, longitude east or west of that point can be calculated. Earliest thinkers measured longitude by comparing the local time of a lunar eclipse at two different places.

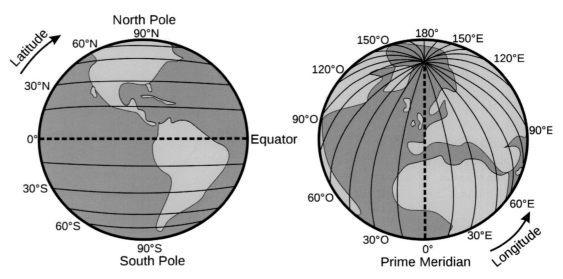

In October 1707, four British men-of-war were returning from the Mediterranean to England. The fleet was under the command of Admiral Sir Cloudesley Shovell, a British hero with a celebrated naval career including the capture of Gibraltar in 1704. As the fleet was surrounded by fog, Admiral Shovell consulted his navigators who agreed they were sailing safely west of the Brittany peninsula in France. They continued north but they were actually heading for the Scilly Isles, some 20 miles south-west of Land's End in Cornwall.

The flagship, HMS *Association*, struck the rocks first and was quickly followed by the other three ships. The exact number of men lost is not known but estimates range from 1400 to 2000, making it one of the worst disasters in the history of the British Navy. The error was attributed to bad weather and the mariners' inability to calculate their longitude correctly. It was clear that something better than dead reckoning was needed to navigate dangerous waters. An accurate method of establishing time in sea conditions was essential.

2.3 Dividing the Circle

The nautical mile is approximately one minute of arc measured along any meridian. By international agreement it has been defined as 1852 metres exactly. It is still used by sea and air navigators worldwide because of its convenience when working with charts. Most nautical charts use the Mercator projection whose scale varies by about a factor of six from the equator to 80 degrees latitude, so charts covering large areas cannot use a single linear scale. The nautical mile is nearly equal to a minute of latitude on a chart, so a distance measured with a chart divider can be roughly converted to nautical miles using the chart's latitude scale.

If we divide a circle into six equal parts using equilateral triangles and then divide each sector into 60 following the sexagesimal system, then we arrive at the angular measure of a degree. The degree can be further divided into 60 minutes of arc, each of which can be divided into 60 seconds. A second of arc is a very small angle and can be visualised as the size of a one-euro coin at a distance of 4.5km. Ground-based astronomers consider themselves lucky if atmospheric fluctuations allow them to see details with a resolution of a few seconds of arc.

We owe our convention of dividing the circle into degrees, minutes and seconds to the Babylonians who inhabited Mesopotamia. The Babylonians used the sexagesimal number base of 60. The number 60, a highly composite number, has 12 factors, namely 1, 2, 3, 4, 5, 6, 10, 12, 15, 20, 30 and 60, two of which, three and five, are prime numbers. With so many factors, many fractions involving sexagesimal numbers are simplified. For example, one hour can be divided evenly into intervals of 30 minutes, 20 minutes, 15 minutes, 12 minutes, 10 minutes, 6 minutes, 5 minutes, 4 minutes, 3 minutes, 2 minutes, and 1 minute.

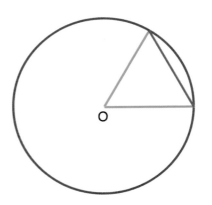

2.04—Dividing the circle into six parts using equilateral triangles.

2.4 Measuring Time

We divide time into hours, minutes and seconds. The origin of the 12-hour day is obscure but may be connected to the 12 signs of the zodiac. Alternatively, it may be due to the custom for people to count on their fingers to 12 using one hand only, with the thumb pointing to each finger bone of the four fingers in turn. A traditional counting system still in use in many regions of Asia works in this way, and could help to explain the occurrence of numeral systems based on 12 and 60.

The hour had been defined by the ancient Egyptians as either one twelfth of daytime or one twelfth of night time, hence both varied with the seasons. Greek astronomers, including Hipparchus and Ptolemy, defined the hour as one twenty-fourth of a mean solar day. In Mediaeval Latin, *pars minuta prima* (first small part) or 'minute' was used for one-sixtieth of a degree, later of an hour. Next in order was *pars minuta secunda,* which became 'second'.

The sundial is the oldest known device for the measurement of time and the most ancient of scientific instruments. It is based on the fact that the shadow of an object will move from one side of an object to the other as the Sun crosses the sky from east to west. The first device for indicating the time of day was probably the gnomon. It consisted of a vertical stick or pillar; the length of its shadow gave an indication of the time of day. The Babylonians and Egyptians built obelisks, slender, tapering four-sided monuments. Their moving shadows formed a kind of sundial, enabling citizens to divide the day into two parts around noon. They also showed the year's longest and shortest days when the shadow at noon was the longest or shortest of the year.

The earliest description of a sundial comes from Berossus, a Babylonian priest. His sundial is a cubical block into which a half-sphere is cut. A small bead is fixed at the centre. During the day the shadow of the bead moves in a circular arc, divided into 12 equal parts. Because the length of the day varies with the season, these hours likewise vary in length from season to season and are thus known as 'temporary hours'.

About AD 100, it was discovered that the shadow cast by a slanting object is a more accurate timekeeper than a shadow cast by a vertical object. If the shadow-casting object is parallel to the Earth's axis, the direction of its shadow at any given hour of the day is constant regardless of the season of the year. In simple modern sundials the style (pronounced *steel*) points to the celestial pole, the point where, if two imaginary lines corresponding to the Earth's axis of rotation were extended, they would intersect with the heavens.

2.05—Amenhotep I, shown on this stele with his mother.

2.5 Water Clocks

The word clock is derived from the celtic words *clocca* and *clogan,* meaning bell. Life in monasteries was well ordered, with time intervals set aside for work, meals, sleep and, of course, daily prayers. Sundials, water clocks or burning candles were used to keep track of time and the bell ringer had the responsibility of regulating the monks' daily routine. It was the bell ringer's job to accurately keep track of time.

It appears that the first water clock was invented in Egypt during the reign of Amenhotep I (1526–1506 BC). Amenhotep's court astronomer, Amenemheb, took credit for creating this device although the oldest surviving mechanism dates to the reign of Amenhotep III. This invention was of great benefit for timekeeping, because the Egyptian hour was not a fixed amount of time but was measured as one twelfth of the night. When the nights were shorter in the summer, these water clocks could be adjusted to measure the shorter hours accurately.

The Tower of the Winds building in Athens was erected about 100–50 BC by Andronicus of Cyrrhus for measuring time. It is an octagonal marble structure 42 feet (12.8 m) high and 26 feet (7.9 m) in diameter. Each of the building's eight sides faces a point of the compass and is decorated with a frieze of figures in relief representing the winds that blow from that direction; below, on the sides facing the Sun, are the lines of a sundial. The Tower was surmounted by a weather vane in the form of a bronze Triton or sea god and contained a water clock (clepsydra) to record the time when the Sun was not shining.

The ancient Greek device known as a clepsydra is literally translated as 'water thief'. This name is actually quite suitable as the water clock measures time by a regulated flow of a liquid from one vessel to another. There are two different types of the water clock based on the flow of the water

2.06—The Tower of the Winds in Athens, built about 100–50 BC to measure time. GEORGE E. KORONAIOS, CREATIVE COMMONS 4.0

being inward or outward to the measuring vessel. Water clocks are known to have existed in ancient Egypt and Babylon as well as in the early civilizations of China and India. Often, they were used side by side with sundials to calibrate each other. On account of its relative accuracy, the water clock was the most widely used time-keeping device until the invention of the pendulum clock in the eighteenth century.

2.6 Sand Glasses and Navigation

The sandglass or hourglass is believed to have originated in mediaeval Europe. Hourglasses were very popular on board ship as, unlike water clocks, they were unaffected by the motion of the ship. They were commonly seen in churches, homes and workplaces until the arrival of mechanical clocks.

Towards the end of the thirteenth century, mechanical clocks started to replace water clocks in churches, cathedrals and public buildings. Falling weights supplied the power and it was controlled by some form of oscillating mechanism like the verge (rod) and foliot (bar) escapement. This type of

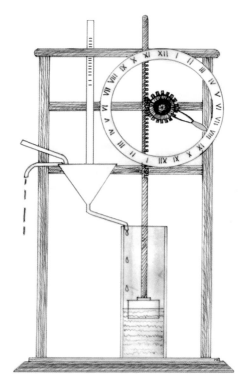

2.07—The mechanism of a water clock that shows the time on a numbered dial.

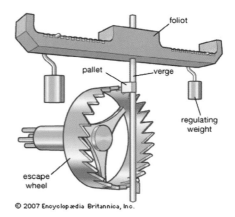

© 2007 Encyclopædia Britannica, Inc.

2.08 (left)—Hourglass. ROYAL MUSEUMS GREENWICH

2.09 (above)—A verge and foliot escapement.

mechanism allowed a gearwheel to advance at a controlled interval or 'tick', measuring the movement of time. The rate of the clock could be adjusted by sliding the weights in or out on the foliot bar.

One of the oldest surviving clocks of this period is in Salisbury Cathedral in the UK. It is thought to date from 1386 and it was restored in 1956. The clock has no dial but it strikes the hours, on each hour. The power is supplied by two large stone weights and as they descend, ropes unwind from two wooden barrels. One barrel drives the main gear, which is regulated by the escapement; the other drives the striking train whose speed is regulated by a fly break. Nowadays, the escapement operates but the striking mechanism has been disabled.

2.8 Galileo and the Pendulum Clock
The idea for the pendulum clock can be traced back to the astronomer Galileo Galilei (1564–1642). Galileo's contribution was essentially theoretical: as a young man in 1582 he noticed that a pendulum swings at a constant rate, at least for small angles. He wrote about this in 1602. At the end of his life, he devised a scheme for using a pendulum to regulate a mechanical clock. Vincenzo Vivani became Galileo's assistant in 1639. He tells us that Galileo as a student observed the behaviour of the pendulum whilst watching a lamp swinging back and forth in Pisa cathedral. He noticed that the time that the lamp took to swing back and forth was independent of the amplitude, the width of its swing; apparently, he measured the period of the swinging lamp with his pulse. When he returned home, he set up two pendulums of equal length and swung one with a large sweep and the other with a small sweep and found that they kept time together. However, the idea of controlling a clock with a pendulum occurred only in his last year. Vivani published a drawing and wrote:

One day in 1641, while I was living with him at his villa in Arcetri, I remember that the idea occurred to him that the pendulum could be adapted to clocks with weights or springs, serving in place of the usual tempo, he hoping that the very even and natural motions of the pendulum would correct all the defects in the art of clocks. But because his being deprived of sight prevented his making drawings and models to the desired effect, and his son Vincenzio coming one day from Florence to Arcetri, Galileo told him his idea and several discussions followed. Finally they decided on the scheme shown in the accompanying drawing, to be put in practice to learn the fact of those difficulties in machines which are usually not foreseen in simple theorizing.

2.10—Galileo Galilei. NATIONAL GALLERY OF ART

There is some evidence that Galileo's son Vincenzio constructed a clock according to this scheme but did not manage to make it work reliably.

In 1665, Christiaan Huygens (1629–1695) built the first pendulum clock. It was far more accurate than any previous clock with an error of only eight seconds in a day. The clock used the traditional verge or crown wheel escapement, powered by a weight. In a pendulum clock the escapement maintains the swing of the pendulum and allows the clock's cogs to advance a fixed amount with each swing, thus moving the hands forward. The oscillating part of a verge escapement needs to swing through a large angle and Huygens realised that if the pendulum swung through such a large angle its timekeeping would suffer. To avoid this problem, he used a pair of gear wheels at the top of his clock to make the verge swing through a larger angle than the pendulum.

2.11—Christiaan Huygens built the first pendulum clock. SCIENCE PHOTO LIBRARY

Christian Huygens (Hugenius).

The formula for the period of a pendulum of length 1 is given by $2\sqrt{(l/g)}$ where g is the acceleration of gravity and is about 9.8 m/s². This means that a pendulum a metre long will have a period of about two seconds and this was usually adopted for longcase clocks. If the amplitude of the pendulum is small, the period will be independent of the amplitude so a long pendulum is better than a short one.

In 1673, Huygens built a clock with a modified pendulum. The top of the pendulum was made of flexible wire that was clamped between curved metal cheeks, altering the pendulum's length as it

2.12—The anchor
escapement.

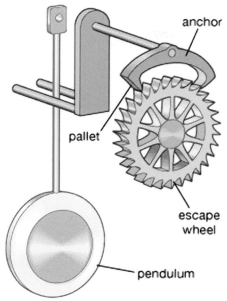

anchor

pallet

escape
wheel

pendulum

swung. By making the cheeks a special shape called a cycloid, Huygens was able to make the time of the swing equal for all amplitudes. As the pendulum could swing through a large angle, there was no need for the gears that had been used in the escapement of the 1656 clock. The first improvement to clock design after the invention of the pendulum was the anchor escapement, which was probably invented by Robert Hooke around 1657, although some references credit clockmaker William Clement (1638–1709). Clement popularized the anchor in his invention of the longcase or grandfather clock around 1680, and disputed credit for the escapement with Hooke. The anchor became the escapement used in almost all pendulum clocks to regulate the swing of the pendulum. Since the pendulum in a clock with an anchor escapement did not need to swing as far as one with a verge escapement, the accuracy was improved and the clock could be enclosed in a case.

The improved accuracy also justified the introduction of the minute hand.

The anchor escapement, like the verge escapement, interferes with the pendulum's motion throughout the whole of its swing, which affects its timekeeping. The 'deadbeat' escapement, invented by Richard Towneley around 1675 and introduced by British clockmaker George Graham FRS (1673–1751) of London in 1715, reduced this problem by giving the pendulum a short impulse

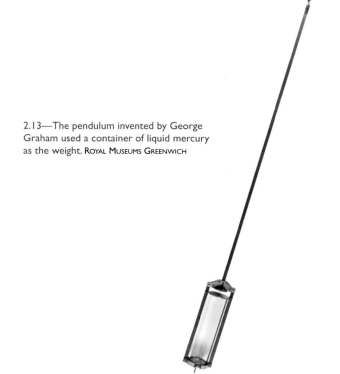

2.13—The pendulum invented by George
Graham used a container of liquid mercury
as the weight. ROYAL MUSEUMS GREENWICH

when it was nearly vertical and allowing it to swing almost freely for the rest of the time.

2.9 Temperature Compensation

The early pendulum clocks were sensitive to temperature changes. A rise in temperature of a metal pendulum caused its length to increase so its period increased and the clock lost time. Wood expands less than metal, so many older quality clocks had wooden pendulum rods. To compensate for this expansion, early high-precision clocks used mercury pendulums, invented by clockmaker George Graham in 1721. These had a bob, or weight, consisting of a container of the liquid metal mercury. An increase in temperature would cause the rod to expand but the mercury in the container would expand also and its level would rise slightly in the container, keeping the centre of gravity of the pendulum at the same height.

The most widely used temperature compensated pendulum was the gridiron pendulum invented by John Harrison in 1726. This consisted of a grid of parallel rods of high thermal-expansion metal such as zinc or brass

33

2.14—John Harrison's gridiron pendulum. ROYAL MUSEUMS GREENWICH

and low thermal-expansion metal such as steel, which was mounted in a frame. It was constructed so that the high expansion rods compensated for the length change of the low-expansion rods, achieving zero length change with temperature changes.

2.10 The Longitude Prize

As a consequence of the disastrous sinking of HMS *Association* and its three sister ships, the British government passed the Longitude Act of 1714, which established the Board of Longitude and offered a prize of £20,000 to anyone who could find a method of determining longitude accurately at sea. The method favoured by astronomers was to use the motion of the Moon through the heavens (or, later, to use Jupiter's satellites) to give the 'absolute' time at a point on the Earth's surface that could be compared with the 'local' time and thereby give the required longitude.

One man who took up the challenge was John Harrison (1693–1776), a carpenter born in West Yorkshire. John and his brother James had already made several ingenious clocks with wooden mechanisms. Harrison's gridiron pendulum enabled his longcase clocks attain an accuracy of one second per month, making them the best timekeepers in existence at that time.

Harrison's first attempt at a 'sea clock' was constructed between 1730 and 1735. On the recommendation of Edmund Halley, the second Astronomer Royal, he was given an interest-free loan by George Graham to support his research. The clock would have to cope with the rolling and pitching motions of a ship so, instead of a pendulum, he used two dumbbell balances linked by

2.15—John Harrison,
carpenter turned
clockmaker. ROYAL MUSEUMS
GREENWICH

2.15—John Harrison,
carpenter turned
clockmaker. ROYAL MUSEUMS
GREENWICH

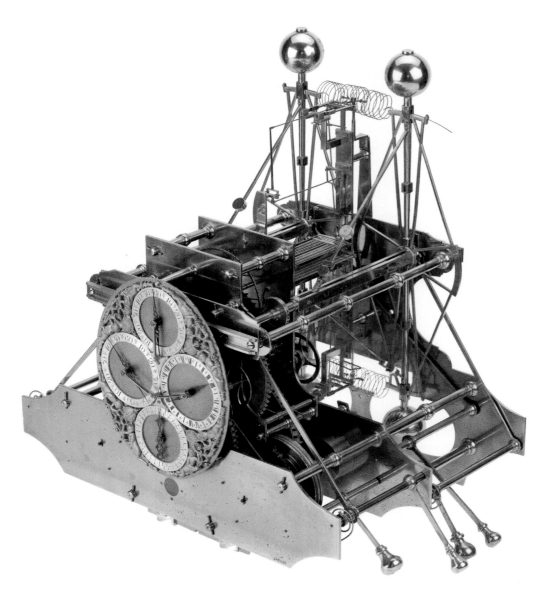

2.16—John Harrison's first sea clock, H1. Royal Museums Greenwich

springs. It was over two feet high and weighed 72 pounds. Harrison demonstrated his clock, H1, to the Royal Society and the Fellows were very impressed. The Board of Longitude considered it worthy of a sea trial so Harrison went on a voyage to Lisbon and back. The clock performed well and the board was impressed enough to grant £500 for further development.

The second sea clock, H2, was similar to H1 but larger and heavier. Harrison worked on it for three years before deciding it would be affected by the motion of a ship. From 1740, he spent 19 years working on H3, which performed well with a following wind but ran slow when the ship was tacking into the wind.

In 1749, Harrison's prestige in the Royal Society was so high that he was awarded the prestigious Copley Medal, the Society's premier award. The citation read by the President, Martin Folkes,

2.17—The third version of John Harrison's sea clock, H3. ROYAL MUSEUMS GREENWICH

2.18—H4, John Harrison's first sea watch. ROYAL MUSEUMS GREENWICH

contained the famous words '… on account of those very curious instruments invented and made by him for the exact mensuration of time'.

Harrison's next attempt, H4, was a large watch with a temperature compensated balance wheel. It was 13cm in diameter and weighed 1.45kg. The balance wheel consisted of a circular bimetallic strip of brass and steel connected to a spiral steel spring; the combination acted as an oscillator. Since Harrison's time an essential component of all mechanical watches has been the balance wheel. As Harrison was now 68 and too frail to undertake a voyage, his son William set sail for the West Indies with H4 on HMS *Deptford* in November 1761. When the ship arrived in Jamaica, the watch was only 5.1 seconds slow, corresponding to 1.25 arc minutes or approximately one nautical mile, and well within the limit required for the prize.

Harrison waited in vain for the £20,000 Longitude Prize. It seemed that the board was reluctant to award it to a mere carpenter and would have preferred that a gentleman won it. Another sea trial was arranged and William set sail for Madeira in March 1764. The astronomer Nevil Maskelyne was also on board the ship to test the Lunar Distance method. On this voyage, H4 was only 39 seconds or 10 miles in error, which was three times better than the accuracy needed to qualify for the prize. Maskelyne's measurements were quite good, with a 30-mile error, but required a considerable amount of calculation. Once again, the board was not satisfied and offered to pay Harrison half of the prize if he revealed the construction of the watch and produced two copies. Harrison reluctantly agreed to these terms and the board asked him to recommend someone to copy H4. He suggested the leading watchmaker Larcon Kendall and was awarded £10,000 as the first half of the prize.

In order to qualify for the second half of the prize, Harrison needed to make two copies of H4 and have them tested. Harrison was now in his seventies and he worked with his son on H5 while Kendall worked on his copy of H4 called K1. The copies H5 and K1 were completed in 1769 and Harrison asked the board to accept them but the board refused.

On 31 January 1772, Harrison, now 79, appealed to George III via a letter to his private astronomer. He was summoned to meet the king who is reported to have said: 'These people have been cruelly wronged and by God I will see them righted'. The king tested H5 himself for ten weeks and found it accurate to a third of a second per day. He advised Harrison to petition parliament for the full prize. Finally, in 1773, aged 80, Harrison received an award of £8,750 for his achievements. He died three years later.

Kendall's watch K1 was used by Captain Cook on his second voyage of discovery to the southern hemisphere. Over the entire three-year voyage, the daily rate of K1 never exceeded eight seconds, corresponding to two nautical miles at the equator. Kendall's second copy, K2, was carried on HMS *Bounty* and travelled with mutineers to Pitcairn Island.

2.11 Solar time and Greenwich Mean Time

The general availability of clocks and watches led to a dilemma: did one use solar time as given by a sundial or clock time? Comparison of sundials and clocks reveals discrepancies of up to 15 minutes either way. This is due to the fact that the Sun does not move across the sky at a constant rate. The orbit of the Earth is slightly elliptical, which means it moves faster when it is closest to the Sun, at perihelion. The shape of the Earth's orbit is given by its eccentricity, the extent to which it is not a perfect circle. In addition, the Earth's spin axis is tilted at an angle of 23.5° to the perpendicular to the orbital plane; this tilt is known as the obliquity and it causes the seasons. The variation of the Earth's eccentricity and obliquity during the year is plotted in red and blue on the adjacent graph. When the two effects are added we get the blue curve, which is known as the equation of time. It is not an equation at all but simply the difference between sundial time and clock time. The black curve crosses the horizontal axis in four places, which shows that sundials and clocks agree four times

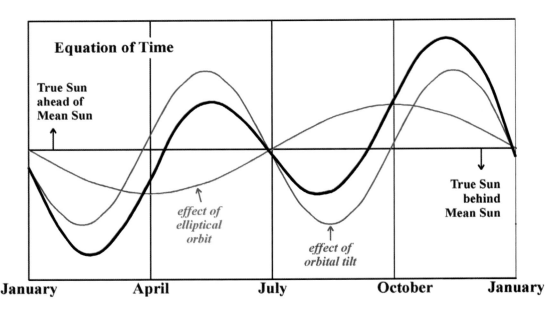

Equation of Time

True Sun ahead of Mean Sun

effect of elliptical orbit

effect of orbital tilt

True Sun behind Mean Sun

January   April   July   October   January

2.19—The equation of time, which shows that time measured by a sundial and by a clock is the same four times a year.

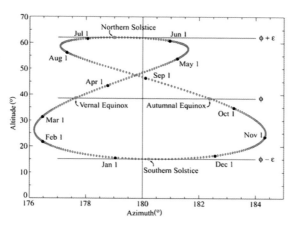

2.20—Analemma diagram
showing the sun's position
in the sky throughout the
year, when taken at the
same time of day from the
same position on earth.

in the year: 16 April, 15 June, 1 September and 25 December. On the other hand, sundials are 14 minutes slow about 12 February and 16 minutes fast about 4 November.

When the Sun's altitude at noon is plotted against its azimuth, or compass bearing, we get a figure-of-eight curve known as an analemma as shown in Fig. 2.20. It gives essentially the same information as the black curve in Fig. 2.19. The first person to capture the Sun's analemma photographically was Dennis di Cocco in 1978–79 as shown in Fig. 2.26.

A clock that runs at a constant rate with each day of the year being 24 hours long shows mean time. It is based on a fictitious entity known as 'the mean sun', which is the average position of the Sun in the sky if the Earth's orbit was circular and the obliquity was zero. For many years clocks displayed the local mean time, which corresponded to the longitude of the place. However, with the coming of the railways from 1830 onwards, the need for a uniform mean time became apparent. The Great Western Railway adopted Greenwich Time in 1847 and other companies soon followed suit. Greenwich Mean Time was adopted officially in the United Kingdom by Act of Parliament on 2 August 1880.

2.12 The International Meridian Conference

In 1884, an international conference was held in Washington DC to determine a prime meridian for international use. Twenty-six nations participated in the International Meridian Conference. The proposal to adopt the meridian passing through the transit instrument at Greenwich Observatory as the prime meridian of longitude was passed 22 to one, two abstaining. San Domingo voted against and France and Brazil abstained. The French did not adopt the Greenwich meridian until 1911. It was also agreed that the mean solar day would begin at midnight on the prime meridian.

2.13 Riefler Clocks

In 1841, Clemens Riefler (1820–76) of Bavaria founded a firm to make drawing instruments and precision clocks. In 1889, his son Sigmund (1847–1912) invented a new form of escapement in which the energy to keep the pendulum swinging is applied by an impulse to a short strip of spring from which the pendulum is suspended. The upper end of the spring is attached to a heavy metal bearer that pivots on two knife edges on its underside. When the pendulum passes its lowest point, the escape wheel is unlocked and pushes the bearer, which pivots slightly on the knife edges and flexes the spring.

Riefler also introduced several innovations that improved the accuracy of their clocks. These included using the low thermal expansion nickel-steel alloy invar for the pendulum. The most accurate models were mounted in a low-pressure tank to eliminate the effect of atmospheric changes on the pendulum. They were powered by a small weight, which was wound up by an electric motor every 30 seconds to avoid the effect of changes in the driving force on the mechanism.

Riefler precision regulator clocks achieved accuracies of a hundredth of a second per day and were used widely in astronomical observatories in the early twentieth century. The first time standard for the United States, provided by the Bureau of Standards (now NIST), was generated by Riefler clocks from 1904 to 1929.

2.14 The Shortt Free Pendulum Clock

The next big advance in timekeeping was made in 1921 by William Hamilton Shortt (1881–1971), a British railway engineer, in collaboration with horologist Frank Hope-Jones (1867–1950), the founder of the Synchronome Company of London. The Shortt clock consists of two separate units: the master pendulum in a copper vacuum tank attached to a wall and a slave-pendulum clock standing a few feet away.

The rod of the master pendulum and its 14-pound bob are made of invar to reduce thermal expansion and contraction. The vacuum tank is evacuated to a pressure of about 30mm of mercury; this eliminates the effect of air resistance on the pendulum. Both pendulums, each about a metre long, have a period of one second, with the slave's rate very slightly slower. Both pendulums are kept swinging by an impulse from the mechanism every 30 seconds. The master and the slave are linked in a feedback loop that keeps the slave synchronised with the master. The rates of the pendulums are compared every 30 seconds and if the slave is lagging it is given an impulse from a spring to speed it up.

About 100 Shortt clocks were manufactured by the Synchronome Company of London and they became the best timekeepers between the 1920s and the 1940s. Professor Hermann Brück installed a Shortt clock (No 86) in Dunsink Observatory in 1954. Daily comparisons with radio time signals gave times accurate to one or two hundredths of a second.

The Shortt was the first clock to be a more accurate timekeeper than the Earth; it was used in 1926 to detect tiny seasonal changes in the Earth's rotation rate. In 1984, Pierre Boucheron studied the accuracy of a Shortt clock belonging to the US National Observatory. He compared its rate with an atomic clock for a month and found it stable to 200 microseconds a day, equivalent to an error rate of one second in 12 years.

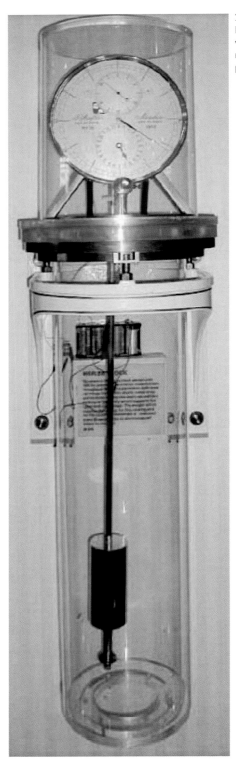

2.21—One of Sigmund Riefler's clock designs in which the pendulum was mounted in a low-pressure tank.

2.22a—Shortt clock used by Dunsink Observatory from 1954.

2.22b—Schematic diagram of a Shortt Free Pendulum Clock.

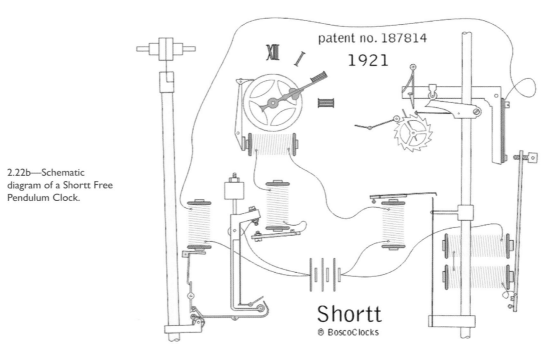

patent no. 187814
1921

Shortt
® BoscoClocks

2.15 Quartz Clocks

The first quartz clock was built in 1927 by Warren Morrison and J.W. Horton at Bell Telephone Laboratories. Quartz is a crystalline form of sand (silicon dioxide) and the crystals exhibit the property of *piezoelectricity,* which means electricity resulting from pressure. Piezoelectricity was discovered in 1880 by French physicists Jacques and Pierre Curie. When a quartz crystal forms part of a suitable circuit it can resonate and provide a constant frequency electrical signal.

2.23—Internal mechanism of a quartz watch.

In clocks and watches the quartz resonator is in the shape of a tuning fork about 3mm long. The crystal is trimmed by a laser to vibrate at a frequency of 32,768Hz or 2^{15} cycles per second. A power of two is chosen so that a simple digital circuit with a chain of divide-by-two stages can provide the one-Hz signal needed to drive the watch's second hand. During the 1970s, the introduction of integrated circuits allowed a small battery to drive either a stepping motor or a liquid crystal display. Since quartz timekeepers can be made very cheaply, they have become the world's most widely-used timekeeping technology and about a billion are sold each year.

In 1929, the US Bureau of Standards (now NIST) made four precision quartz oscillators operating at 100kHz. The large crystals were contained in temperature-controlled ovens to prevent frequency drift due to the thermal expansion of the large quartz resonators. These quartz oscillators became the basis for the US standard of time between the 1930s and the 1960s.

2.16 Relativity and Quantum Mechanics

In his theory of Special Relativity, the physicist Albert Einstein showed that space and time are closely intertwined and that we live in a four-dimensional 'spacetime' universe.

For normal activities, where relative speeds are small compared to the velocity of light, there is a clear distinction between three spatial dimensions and one time dimension. However, cosmonauts travelling in two spacecraft travelling at relative speeds comparable with the velocity of light (299,792.458 km/s or a billion feet per second) will find that the other guy's spacecraft appears to have contracted in its direction of motion and its clocks are going slow. The situation becomes really bizarre if the spacecraft venture near a black hole.

In the 1960s, John Wheeler (1911–2008) and Bryce DeWitt (1911–2004) tried to apply Erwin Schrödinger's equation governing the wave function

2.24—Albert Einstein.

2.25—Belfast-born physicist John S. Bell.

of quantum mechanical systems to Einstein's General Theory of Relativity and they came up with a result known as the Wheeler-DeWitt Equation. Unfortunately, time has no role in this equation. Then in 1983, Don Page and William Wooters provided a solution based on the quantum phenomenon of entanglement. When a measurement is made on one member of a pair of entangled particles, the other member of the pair is always found to have the appropriately correlated value. Thus, there is a correlation between the results of measurements on entangled pairs even if they are separated by very large distances that preclude communication at the speed of light. Einstein called entanglement 'spooky action at a distance' but John S. Bell (1928–1990), the Belfast-born theoretical physicist, showed it was possible.

In 2013, Ekaterina Moreva at the Istituto Nazionale di Ricera Metrologica (INRIM) in Turin

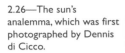

2.26—The sun's analemma, which was first photographed by Dennis di Cicco.

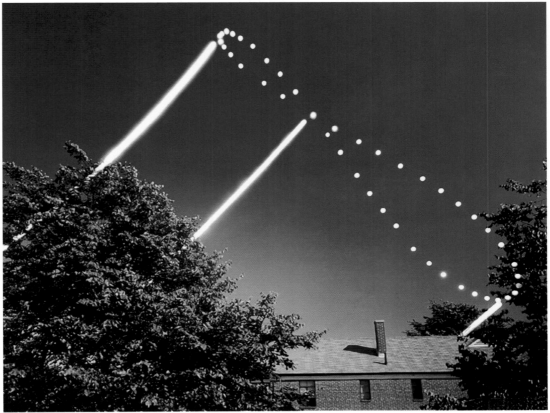

and five colleagues carried out the first experimental test of Page and Wooter's idea. Their experiment consisted in measuring the polarisation of laser beams in two different configurations. The results suggest that time is an emergent property of entanglement. Time will tell if they are right.

2.17 Improvements in Timekeeping

Great advances were made in the design of clocks and watches over several years. However, the application of scientific knowledge in the twentieth century brought even greater progress and those early clockmakers would be amazed at the technology that is readily available in the twenty-first century. These advances are discussed in Chapter 6.

3. The Time Ball and the Ballast Office clock

Mad Dogs and Englishmen, go out in the midday sun.
The smallest Malay rabbit deplores this stupid habit.
In Hong Kong, they strike a gong, and fire off a noonday gun.
To reprimand each inmate, who's in late.
Mad Dogs and Englishmen by Noel Coward (1899–1973)

3.1 Time Balls and Time Guns

The invention of the marine chronometer realised the possibility of using clocks for navigation. If a ship carried a chronometer showing mean time at a particular longitude, say the Royal Observatory in Greenwich, London, then observations of the Sun, Moon or stars provided the ship's local time and hence its longitude relative to Greenwich.

The first practical chronometer for use at sea, named H4, was made by John Harrison (1693–1776) in 1760 and it eventually won him the Longitude Prize. In France, Pierre Le Roy introduced innovations that made his chronometers more reliable and independent of temperature variations. His masterpiece of 1766 equalled the performance of Harrison's H4 but was expensive to produce. In England, Thomas Earnshaw (1749–1829) and John Arnold (1736–1799) made further improvements. Arnold's design facilitated production in quantity at a reasonable price.

3.01—John Harrison's H4, his first practical timekeeper for use at sea, was designed as a large watch. Royal Museums Greenwich

By 1825, the Royal Navy routinely equipped its ships with chronometers, which assured its supremacy over the Portuguese, Dutch and French navies. It is no exaggeration to say that the chronometer was one of the foundation stones of the British Empire.

In order to transmit mean time to ships offshore, a Scottish man, Capt. Robert Wauchope of the Royal Navy, invented the time ball. It was a large wooden or metal

45

3.02—The use of chronometers on board its ships helped assure British naval supremacy. BJOERTVEDT, CREATIVE COMMONS

3.03—The time ball installed at Greenwich Royal Observatory in 1833. TILMAN 2007, CREATIVE COMMONS

3.04—The time ball atop the Nelson Monument at Calton Hill, Edinburgh.
JONATHAN OLDENBUCK, CREATIVE COMMONS

ball that was dropped at a predetermined time to enable the sailors to check their chronometers. The first time ball was erected at Portsmouth, England, in 1829 and was followed by others at major ports. In 1833, a time ball was installed at the Royal Observatory, Greenwich, by the Astronomer Royal, John Pond, and the ball has been dropped at 1 p.m. every day since then.

At Edinburgh, a time ball was erected in 1852 on top of the Nelson Monument on Calton Hill. The system was designed by clockmaker Frederick James Ritchie in collaboration with Professor Charles Piazzi Smyth, the Astronomer Royal for Scotland. The time ball was so successful that there was a demand for an audible signal on foggy days and, from 1861, a gun was fired at 1 p.m. from Edinburgh Castle. The master clock on Calton Hill was linked by an electric cable to a clock at the castle to enable the gun to be fired automatically. A map was produced to show the actual time when the sound of the gun reached various places across Edinburgh. For instance, the time lag for the port of Leith was 11 seconds. The story is told that the practice of firing the gun on Sundays was discontinued as the moment it was fired there was quite a little stir in church by everyone checking their watches. A team of volunteers still fires the 1 p.m. gun and the ceremony is a popular tourist attraction. Edinburgh's professional rugby team, *The Gunners*, take their nickname from this daily ritual. The firm of Ritchie of Edinburgh still exists and is responsible for maintaining the system and the famous Edinburgh Floral Clock.

3.05—Firing the 1pm gun at Edinburgh Castle.

3.2 Plans for a Dublin Time Service

The first mention of a time ball in the Dublin port archives is a letter dated 28 February 1865 from Yeates & Son of 2 Grafton Street to Robert Caldwell, a member of the Ballast Board. Yeates presented the board with a 1/12 scale model of a time ball and its electromagnetic release mechanism. The six-inch brass ball was raised by a string and pulley mechanism and was released by a signal to a double coil. The model was in the possession of the Royal Dublin Society until February 1990 when it was stolen. Yeates' specification for the real time ball was:

> The ball to be made of copper 4 or 5 feet in diameter, the mast 15 feet high and 6 inches square, composed of three pieces of deal, bolted together and surmounted by a wind vane and letters of the cardinal points. The windlass for hoisting rapidly or slowly at pleasure.

At its meeting on 10 March, the board members considered a report from Robert Caldwell and

3.06—The original model of the Ballast Office time ball devised by Yeates & Son, instrument makers.

presumably they viewed Yeates' model. Caldwell recommended:

> … a clock of the best construction placed in the lower part of the house [the Ballast Office], which ball shall be disengaged at the precise point of time with perfect regularity by means of a small coil, the machinery of which can be enclosed in a glass case for safety. I have no doubt that the Board of Trinity College would allow us to check the rate of the clock from time to time, by the aid of the Transit instrument in the Fellows Garden. (This is a reference to the magnetic observatory that was established in 1838 by Humphrey Lloyd as Dublin's contribution to a great international effort to study the Earth's magnetism.)

Caldwell estimated that the clock would cost about 80 guineas and the rest of the apparatus about £57. The board resolved 'that the Dock Committee who will shortly have to visit London be directed to carry the recommendation of the report, taking care that all appliances be of the most perfect description'.

3.3 The Start of the Time Service

On 3 November 1865, the *Freeman's Journal* reported that extensive alterations and improvements had been completed at the Ballast Office premises. The report continued:

> This office has been furnished with one of Dent's improved clocks, a costly and wonderful piece of mechanism, replete with every modern application of science. The time ball, visible on the external angle of the parapet, has been arranged by means of an electric current in connection with this clock, to fall daily at twelve o'clock [sic] precisely, to give the true time to mariners. The manner in which all details have been perfected of this ingenious means of denoting the correct hour each day reflects much credit on the optician, Mr Yeates.

3.07—A time ball with its pulley and rope hoisting mechanism on the roof of the Equitable Life Assurance Society building in Boston, United State, in 1881. CREATIVE COMMONS

In fact, two clocks were involved. The 'improved clock' was a Dent pendulum clock (No 1290) with mercury compensation and a sliding rate adjustment and it was installed in the board room. Its mechanism could go for 12 months on one winding and its performance corresponded to changes of the rate of less than 0.1 seconds per day. It cost £125.

A second clock, made by Booth Brothers of Dublin, drove the dial on the front of the building and was known as the 'Front Clock'.

The Ballast Office Clock was the most accurate public clock in Dublin at the time and it became a popular rendezvous point for people – 'Meet you under the Ballast Office Clock' was a well-known saying in Dublin.

3.08—The Dent 12-month pendulum clock installed in the Ballast Office.

Yeates & Son, founded in 1728, was one of the foremost instrument-making firms in Dublin at that time and the owner was Stephen Mitchell Yeates (1832–1901). Stephen had inherited the firm from his father Samuel (1762–1834) and his brother George (1796–1862). On Stephen's death, the firm was run by Arthur Mitchell Yeates, the only surviving son. The firm made and sold a great range of scientific instruments and from 1852 to 1910 its advertisements included 'Instrument Makers to the University', which implies that Trinity College was a good customer. Although no family members were involved, from 1940 the firm of Yeates & Sons continued as ophthalmic opticians in the Grafton Street area until the year 2000.

Some records indicate that the time ball was completed in February 1868 and started operation in 1870 but the exact date is not clear from the records. The total cost was about £96. Contrary to the *Freeman's Journal* report, the ball was released initially at 1 p.m. Dunsink Time.

3.4 Franz Friedrich Brünnow: 3rd Royal Astronomer

By April 1866, a new Royal Astronomer was in residence at Dunsink Observatory following the death of Sir William Rowan Hamilton on 2 September 1865. The Observatory, located north-west of the Phoenix Park, had been established by Trinity College in 1783 for astronomical research and from 1866 it provided a time service to the Ballast Board to regulate the accurate dropping of the time ball.

The new Royal Astronomer was Dr Franz Brünnow of German origin who had been the first director of the Detroit Observatory and who introduced German astronomical methods to America. Brünnow was a skilled observer and, while at Detroit Observatory, had transmitted regular time

3.09—Dunsink Observatory. David Malone, DAVID MALONE, CREATIVE COMMONS

3.10—Sir William Rowan Hamilton, the brilliant mathematician, who was appointed Royal Astronomer of Ireland in 1827.

3.11—Dr Franz Brünnow who initiated Dunsink Observatory's role in sending a signal to release the time ball.

signals to the neighbouring cities of Detroit and Milwaukee. In a letter dated 28 April to William Lees, who was then secretary to the Ballast Board, Brünnow expressed his willingness to supply the time for regulating a time ball 'as often as you desire'. This could be done either by sending a couple of chronometers to Dunsink or by using a telegraphic connection. The former method was adopted at first.

The next significant development was B.B. Stoney's report to the board of 15 November 1866 on methods for checking and controlling clocks. After apologising for the delay in obtaining the information, he outlined three systems:

> Transport of chronometers between a mean time clock in a local observatory and the controlled clock. This method was inferior to either of the others.
>
> The controlled clock is connected by electric wire to a mean time clock in a local observatory. This system was used in Glasgow to control 16 clocks and the regulation was perfectly satisfactory. Similar systems were in use in Edinburgh and Liverpool. He estimated the cost of a telegraph line from Dunsink to the Ballast Office at £120 with an annual rental of twelve guineas.

The third plan, which was in use in Newcastle, was to receive a time signal from Greenwich at 10 a.m. each morning. The Astronomer Royal, Sir George Airy, had recommended the Electric and International Telegraph Company as reliable. A Dublin clockmaker, Mr Moore, had offered to supply the correct time by current from Greenwich and to let fall the time ball every day, except Sunday, for £130 p.a.

Following the establishment of the Dublin Port and Docks Board in 1867, Nicholas Proud was appointed its secretary and he was responsible for the day-to-day operation of the time service for the next 54 years. He had been employed by the Ballast Board from 1862.

3.5 The Automation of the Dunsink Time Service

Meanwhile, the Port and Docks Board had been considering the improvement of the Dunsink system by introducing a telegraph line between the Observatory and the Ballast Office. In November 1873, the TCD Registrar informed Nicholas Proud that 'the College have recently erected a Transit at Dunsink which is probably the best of its kind'. This was the Pistor and Martins Circle made in Berlin and similar to the instrument that Brünnow had used 20 years earlier in Ann Arbor. A transit circle is a telescope for observing the passage or transit of an astronomical body across the meridian position, or circle, of the observer. By recording the seconds beat of a sidereal clock, in which time is measured in terms of the Earth's motion relative to fixed stars, transits could be measured to an accuracy of one or two hundredths of a second of time. The Registrar also mentioned that the College would attend to the scientific part of the project if the board supplied a telegraph line.

Proud immediately applied to the Post Master General for a private wire from Dunsink to the Ballast Office. He pointed out that a time service for the city was a matter of great public interest and expressed the hope the government would assist them by ordering the wire to be laid free of charge. On 31 December, the Surveyor of Private Wires wrote to Mr Proud to inform him that his application for a free wire had been refused and the board would have to pay the annual rental of £30-10-0. The telegraph seems to have been in place by April 1873 but Mr Proud delayed paying the rental in the hope that a renewed application for a free line might be successful. The Post Office reminded him that he had already signed a contract and the rental was due.

By May 1873, the dropping of the time ball each weekday was being controlled electrically from Dunsink. About five minutes before 1 p.m. Dublin Time, the ball was raised to the top of the pole on the roof of the Ballast Office and engaged a catch. At 1 p.m. precisely the signal from Dunsink released the catch, causing the ball to fall under gravity. The mariners used the first movement of the ball to correct the rate of their chronometers. On the whole, the system was very reliable. The main difficulty for the Dunsink observers was bad weather, which meant that they might not be able to observe the transits of stars for several days. The telegraph line was prone to damage from falling branches and interference by the Post Office engineers. At the Ballast Office, a variety of causes could sometimes prevent the ball being always released at the correct time.

The slave clock in the Ballast Office was a 28-day Dent bought for £25 in 1873 and modified by Yeates. It also controlled the famous 'Front' clock on the Westmoreland Street façade of the Ballast Office. As well as controlling the time ball, the single strand of copper wire from Dunsink was connected in series to slave clocks in the Ballast Office, the Bank of Ireland in College Green and the Museum Building in Trinity College where it went to Earth.

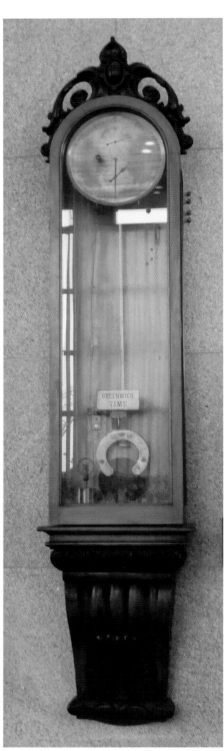

3.12—The Dent slave clock in the Ballast Office controlled the front clock on Westmoreland Street.

3.13 —The Booth slave clock in the Trinity College Museum Building was also controlled from Dunsink.

The slave clocks of the Dunsink Time Service differed from the RDS slave clocks in that the wooden pendulums of the slave clocks had bobs consisting of pairs of permanent horseshoe magnets that swung past fixed coils carrying the timing signals. Each master clock and each slave clock had a 'tell-tale' indicator, which showed the flow of the electrical pulses and their polarity. The electrical current was maintained by a battery of Daniell cells.

When the Pistor and Martins Circle was installed in 1873, Professor Brünnow subjected it to a comprehensive investigation. Unfortunately, he had to resign in 1874, aged 53, because of failing eyesight.

3.14—The pendulum bob of the Ballast Office slave clock.

3.6 Robert Stawell Ball: 4th Royal Astronomer

Brünnow was succeeded by 34-year-old Robert Stawell Ball. The new Andrews Professor made several immediate improvements to the instrumentation in Dunsink. He replaced the Arnold clocks with a Dent sidereal clock (No 2032) in 1875 and a Booth mean time master clock in 1876. The Dent clock had a mercury compensated pendulum and is still in working order at Dunsink. The Booth clock was provided with electrical contacts so it could be used as a master mean time clock for the Time Service. Both clocks appear to have worked very satisfactorily.

On 4 February 1881, Francis M. Moore, a clockmaker of 25 Eden Quay, wrote to the Port and Docks Board claiming that the time ball was inaccurate. He offered to take over the equipment and

3.15—The Dent sidereal clock still in working order at Dunsink Observatory.

3.16—Sir Howard Grubb.

guaranteed accurate release of the ball for £15 per annum. He wrote also to Captain Kiddle, R.N., principal officer of the Board of Trade in Dublin, and gave the time of fall on five days between 28 February and 9 March. One of these was on time, one was not wound up and the other three were 64 to 67 seconds too late. The letter was forwarded to London and a Whitehall official asked if the board was investigating the allegations. The board sent copies to 'Dr Ball and Yeates & Co.'.

Professor Ball replied: 'While I regret to hear that errors in the signal have been complained of I have to state that we are in no way responsible for them'. He gave an extract from the Dunsink journal to show that the time signals left Dunsink within one second of the correct time. He suggested that Howard Grubb of the Grubb Telescope Company be consulted on a 'really effective mechanism for releasing the time ball' and that a daily record should be kept of its performance. Yeates denied that the mechanism was defective and offered to carry out a daily inspection and winding for £12 per annum. This contract was accepted with effect from 1 April 1881.

3.7 Robert Ball is Knighted

On 11 January 1886, Professor Ball received the following letter from Lord Carnarvon, who was then Lord Lieutenant:

> The eminent services which you have rendered to science and to education will, I hope, justify in your eyes the proposal I am about to make. It would give me great pleasure to confer upon you the honour of a knighthood – if, as I trust, this should be acceptable to you. May I add that in proposing this public recognition of high service, I am making it not only to the Astronomer Royal, [sic] but to the Professor of Astronomy in the University of Dublin.

The ceremony was duly performed at Dublin Castle on 23 January.

Over a period of 17 months from January 1888, Yeates wrote four times to defend their care of the clocks in response to complaints from Nicholas Proud. They blamed snow and frost and repairs to the telegraph line. Their letter of 23 May 1899 suggested the most probable cause of the failure of the ball to fall was: 'Some minute particles of dust falling between the points at the moment of contact'. In response the board minuted the action: 'Inform Mr Yeates that the board cannot consider their explanation satisfactory and must place the matter in other hands if any further irregularities occur'.

The irregularities must have continued as Sir Robert Ball wrote on 10 Dec 1890:
> I have had under consideration your recent communication relative to the time service between Dunsink Observatory and the Port and Docks Board. ... Although no reliable information of a definitive character has been furnished to me yet I hear that irregularities have been alleged to exist in the clocks in Dublin which are connected to the system. ... I have come to the conclusion that the divided responsibility must terminate. ... I would therefore suggest that the Port and Docks Board should provide a competent inspector under my control as to duties, appointment and dismissal. ... It will thus be seen that I am writing to continue the time service provided that entire responsibility for carrying it out is entrusted to me.

During a temporary absence of Sir Robert from Dunsink, his assistant, Arthur Rambaut, wrote

3.17—Arthur Alcock Rambaut appointed fifth Royal Astronomer in 1892.

3.18—Prof. Robert Stawell Ball. ROYAL ASTRONOMICAL SOCIETY/SCIENCE PHOTO LIBRARY

to Nicholas Proud on 27 January 1891:

> Yours of yesterday convinces me that, as I was of the opinion all through, the principal part of any errors which may have occurred in the dropping of your time ball are due to a want of attention of the clocks in town. … As matters are at present when anything occurs Mr Yeates says we are responsible for it and we say that he is and there appears to be nobody competent to find out which of us is at fault.

On 18 February 1891, Sir Robert sent to the Board a suggested form of diary similar to that used at Dunsink to be kept at the Ballast Office to record the performance of the clocks. This letter, which is the first in the archive to be typewritten and the earliest typewritten letter from Dunsink that survives, indicates the signalling system in use at that time. As well as the drop-second at one second each minute from Dunsink there was a return signal each minute at '8 secs'. There was also a half-hour return signal lasting for a few seconds that told Dunsink the state of the boardroom clock and a signal to indicate the correct falling of the time ball. In the next letter dated 10 March, Sir Robert suggests that William, his son, then due to start in Trinity, should be employed as clock inspector. William probably took up his duties in May 1891.

During March 1891, Yeates carried out modifications to the Ballast Office clocks and the time ball to enable better monitoring of the system. In May the Dunsink circuit was temporarily disconnected from the TCD and RDS clocks and earthed at the Ballast Office. This allowed thorough testing of the return signals to Dunsink.

A signed statement of 1 June 1892 lists 'Duties of Inspector of Board's Clocks':

> I undertake the winding of the clocks in the Street and connected one in the

Boardroom and to inspect and see that the time is correct every morning (Sundays excepted). To inspect weekly the inspecting apparatus, keeping all in perfect order and to be responsible for the time ball falling to time as signalled from Dunsink for the yearly sum of £12. Signed W.V. Ball, The Observatory, Dunsink, Co. Dublin, 1st June 1892.

On 20 February 1892, Sir Robert learned that he had been successful in his application for the chair of Lowndean Professor at Cambridge. He relished the prospect of lighter teaching duties and the intellectual stimulation of Cambridge. In a lighter vein he wrote to his sister: 'Yes, it is a great affair! I suppose it is the highest scientific chair in England, if not in Europe, the Solar System, the Milky Way, or the Universe!' Sir Robert wrote his last report to the TCD board in June and by the autumn he had started to lecture in Cambridge.

3.8 Arthur Alcock Rambaut: 5th Royal Astronomer

The TCD board elected Arthur Alcock Rambaut as the 5th Royal Astronomer on 22 October. He had been assistant since 1882 and was the only one to be promoted to the Andrews Professorship. With his wife and two sons he moved from the assistant's house to the main observatory building. A third son was born in 1894.

On 27 October 1892, Professor Rambaut wrote to Nicholas Proud:

I should be glad if you would now make some permanent arrangement for the superintendence of your clocks, as my duties at the Observatory and in College will occupy my whole time. The arrangement which Sir R. Ball was led to adopt about a year ago under which his son superintended the clocks and reported their performance to him seems the most suitable one. … If the Board approves of my proposal to continue the arrangement introduced by Sir Robert Ball I would suggest Mr Charles Longford as a suitable person for the post. He is the son of the late Mr Longford [John Henry Longford] of [10] Westmoreland Street and is at present mechanical assistant to Mr Stanley (dentist) who succeeded his father. Being there on the spot it would be little trouble to him to look after the clocks and he would be willing to undertake the task for the same salary as Mr Ball was in receipt of. He is quite familiar with the system of clock which we employ at the Observatory, where he has often helped me in my work, and is to be thoroughly relied on in anything he undertakes.

Charles Longford's familiarity with the Dunsink instruments stemmed from the fact that Rambaut's wife, Emily, was his sister, some nine years older, and Charles probably was a frequent visitor to the Rambaut family.

Professor Rambaut had second thoughts about his proposal and wrote on 28 November:

On thinking over the matter I came to the conclusion that it would be better, if anything in the nature of a formal agreement is necessary, that I should undertake it and that Mr Longford should remain responsible to me. … If you entrust the care of your clocks to me I will undertake to keep them running with the standard mean time clock at the Observatory, to have them examined every day, wound up and their performance reported to me every week, in consideration of the sum [of] £12 a year to be paid to a person I shall recommend and your Board approve of (in the present instance Mr Longford) and that this person shall be considered as my representative in the matter and be responsible only to me. This last point I consider very important.

A signed statement of 9 December runs as follows:

> I undertake to have the clock in the street and the clock connected in the Board Room regularly wound, and to have inspected and seen that the time is correct every morning (Sundays excepted). To have inspected weekly clock apparatus, keeping all in perfect order, and to be responsible for the Time Ball falling to time, as signalled from Dunsink, for the yearly sum of twelve pounds (£12) sterling. (Signed) Arthur A. Rambaut

In December also, Yeates carried out repairs to the Booth 'Front' or street clock as recommended by Rambaut.

In February 1893, Howard Grubb wrote on behalf of the RDS to Nicholas Proud requesting permission to attach a light spring to the release mechanism of the time ball so that the fall of the ball could be signalled to Leinster House, which housed the RDS at the time. Permission was granted. The RDS system had been terminated a couple of years earlier but the clocks in Leinster House still needed to be regulated. It seems that the signal from the Ballast Office to the RDS actuated the little model of the time ball that Yeates had made in 1865.

The 'Front' clock on the Westmoreland Street façade of the Ballast Office was a major source of the errors that occurred and it caused Professor Rambaut to write to Nicholas Proud on 21 February 1893:

3.19—The Ballast Office Front clock on the Westmoreland Street façade. DUBLIN PORT ARCHIVE

ONE DUBLIN DAY

Cleaning the Ballast Office Clock, Westmoreland Street.

It has been felt for some time that the present plan, by which the Trinity College Clock in the New Buildings [now called the Museum Building] is controlled by your front clock, is not a satisfactory one. The latter, although much improved by the alterations you have made, is not by any means a suitable clock to be controlled on the system we employ; much less to control another which being of the highest workmanship, and enclosed in a tightly fitting case is susceptible of the greatest precision. ... I am therefore authorised to ask your Board's consent to have the clock in the New Buildings put on the direct circuit from Dunsink so that Trinity College may get its time directly from its own Observatory. ... This will not in any way interfere with your two clocks; it only means that the line after passing through your clocks, instead of going to earth directly, will pass through the one clock in College and go to earth there and the change will not I believe introduce any irregularity in the running of your clocks.

Permission was granted.

Charles Longford became sick in December 1892 and was replaced until May 1895 by Reginald Tyrrell, son of Robert Y. Tyrrell, Regius Professor of Greek in Trinity College.

In 1897, Professor Rambaut became director of the Radcliffe Observatory where he co-operated with Howard Grubb in installing a large double refractor with a 24-inch photographic lens and an 18-inch visual lens. The telescope was used successfully for measuring stellar parallaxes photographically.

3.20—Prof. Charles Jasper Joly.

3.9 Charles Jasper Joly: 6th Royal Astronomer

Rambaut was succeeded by Charles Jasper Joly, aged 33, from Trinity, an expert in the mathematical methods of quaternions.

3.10 The Saga of the Dunsink Telephone

Before Professor Rambaut left for Oxford he suggested to the Port and Docks Board that a telephone at Dunsink would be a great convenience for sorting out time service problems. He wrote in a letter to Nicholas Proud on 8 May 1897 and after commenting on the high efficiency of the service over the past half year continues:

> … On two occasions the time was interrupted by trees falling across [the telegraph line] but these accidents were not allowed to interfere very long with the control of the clocks through the energy of my assistant [Charles Martin] who went into town and set the linesman to repair the line without delay. It would however be a great convenience to us if we had a telephone to the Observatory by means of which we could communicate with the Post Office when such accidents occur and have them set right at once. … I find that the annual expense would only amount to 12 guineas annually as soon as the proposed exchange is opened at Castleknock. Of course I would not expect the Port and Docks Board to bear the whole expense of such a telephone which would naturally be used for other purposes also. But in view of the fact that we have, without any remuneration, been supplying you with the correct time for about a quarter of a century at considerable inconvenience and that a telephone would render the service much less troublesome and anxious, I think I might fairly ask the Board to contribute something – say one third or 4 guineas annually to the expense. I should be very much obliged if you would bring the matter to the notice of the Board at their next meeting.
>
> I remain, Yours very truly, Arthur A. Rambaut
>
> P.S. To meet a possible objection I might add that the telephone line will come direct to Castleknock and thence to the Observatory by quite a different route from that followed by the existing line. The chances therefore of both being interrupted accidently at the same time is almost nil.

Professor Rambaut wrote again on 17 May to enquire if Nicholas Proud had brought his last letter to the notice of the board and whether any decision had been come to with regard to it.

There is no mention of the telephone in the archive for over a year until The National Telephone Company Ltd. quoted the rental for three options on 30 June 1898:

Dunsink to the Dublin Exchange:	£26-0-0 p.a.
Dunsink to the Glasnevin Exchange:	£18-10-0 p.a.
Dunsink to the Castleknock Exchange:	£ 11-0-0 p.a.

The following day, 1 July, Mr Proud received an irate letter from the TCD Registrar:

> The Astronomer Royal [sic] [then Professor Joly] having represented to the Board of Trinity College that, in consequence of repeated failure of the ball apparatus, he should feel obliged to recommend discontinuance of the Time service unless the Port and Docks Board supplied Dunsink Observatory with a telephone, I am directed to request

3.21—Nicholas Proud, secretary of the Dublin Port and Docks Board.

your Board to supply same, the Board of TCD having given Astronomer Royal's [sic] service gratuitously.

The same day Mr Proud also received a letter from Professor Joly expressing satisfaction with the £11 p.a. estimate.

On 5 July, The National Telephone Company sent agreement forms to Mr Proud and mentioned that they were '… at present engaged in opening an exchange at Castleknock and we could connect you with Dublin via this exchange for the annual rental of £11'. As nothing happened for six months, the Castleknock exchange was probably still under construction.

On 1 February 1899 Professor Joly wrote to Mr Proud:

I shall be glad if you will draw the attention of your Board to the letter dated 30 June, 1889 from the Registrar of Trinity College Dublin, relating to the present state of the Time Service. At present when anything goes astray with the clocks or with the time ball at the Ballast Office, my assistant or I immediately go into town in order to have the defect made right by Mr Yeates that the ball may fall at the proper time. Last year we had to go into town on fifteen different occasions solely on this account. These interruptions, besides being most inconvenient, interfere with the regular work of calculation and reduction of astronomical observations carried out at the Observatory. It was in consequence of my report to the Visitors on this matter at the last Visitation at the Observatory, that the letter of the Registrar was written.

You will please mention to the Board that the Telephone Company estimate the cost of a telephone at £11 per annum while the Port and Docks Board at present pay £12 per annum for the inspection of the clocks. This inspection would be unnecessary if the telephone were provided because, by means of the return signal by the telegraph wire, we are able at Dunsink to detect immediately any irregularity. In my opinion the Time Service would be much more efficient than at present if we had a telephone. I may mention that no failure or irregularity of the time ball during the past year was due to any defect of the instruments at Dunsink. The failures were entirely owing to defects in the instruments at the Ballast Office or to the breaking of the telegraph wire in the recent storm.

Yours faithfully, C.J. Joly (Royal Astronomer of Ireland)

On 10 February, Professor Joly wrote to Mr Proud: 'I am obliged for your letter announcing that your Board agree to my proposal about the telephone'. On 17 February, Mr Proud signed an agreement for the supply of a telephone line from Dunsink to the Castleknock exchange for £11 p.a. The pro forma receipt from G.W. Gwyther, district manager of the telephone company, stated: 'The necessary work has been put in hand and will be finished as soon as possible'.

On 20 April 1899, G.W. Gwyther wrote to Mr Deane, assistant secretary of the Port and Docks Board:

In reference to your letter of the 18th inst I beg to say that we have been unable to complete the line to Dunsink Observatory owing to the fact that the Postmaster General has withheld his consent to crossing the Midland Great Western Railway near Ashtown. I shall be greatly obliged if your Board can bring any pressure to bear on the Post Office as they have exclusive rights over these Railways. I am sure that the question in the House [of Commons] addressed to Mr Hanbury would have a very helpful effect.

On 5 May, Professor Joly wrote to Mr Proud:

I am obliged for your letter announcing your satisfactory arrangement with the Post Office. I suggested to Mr Deane that the Port and Docks Board should retain Mr Longford's services until the telephone was ready. I have said nothing to Mr Longford on the subject as I was not aware for what period his services would be required.

On 6 May 1899, G.W. Gwyther wrote to Mr Proud:

With reference to your letter of the 5th inst I beg to say that since mine of the 20th April we have received from the Postmaster General permission to cross the Railway; this being the case we have now applied to the Midland Great Western Railway for their consent and expect to receive it any day.

On 13 June 1899, Professor Joly wrote to Mr Proud:

I shall be obliged if you will let me know the present state of your negotiations with the Telephone Company in order that I may report on the matter to the Visitors at the Annual Visitation of the Observatory on June 20th.

On 7 July 1899, Professor Joly wrote to Mr Proud:

I shall be obliged if you will note that the Telephone Company has not yet furnished a report as to the progress of the telephone connection to the Observatory. I presume you will make temporary arrangements with Mr Longford.

On 10 July, G.W. Gwyther wrote to Mr Proud:
With reference to your letter of 7th inst to hand today, I beg to say that the cause of the delay in running wire to the Dunsink Observatory is difficulty in obtaining permission to carry the line along the public road but we have almost succeeded in obtaining permission over private property when if we are successful the wire will be very shortly completed.

On 7 November 1899, G.W. Gwyther wrote to Mr Proud:
Your favour of the 4th inst. We have great and unexpected difficulty in getting permission to carry the wire across property and along roads in that neighbourhood. We have however succeeded in doing so and will complete this wire as soon as the repairs after the last storm are completed, say in about a month or six weeks.

On 8 November, Professor Joly wrote to Mr Proud:
I enclose a letter received today from the Telephone Company stating that they have now overcome the difficulties about wayleave but that on account of the late storm they will not have the wire completed for a month or six weeks. I do not think this quite satisfactory.

On 10 January 1900, G.W. Gwyther wrote to Mr Proud:
I am obliged by your letter of 6th inst and beg to say that owing to the storm which occurred in November we were unable to complete the wire as arranged as on the whole our staff were employed in restoring the service. This wire will however be started on Monday the 15th inst and completed without further delay.

On 17 March 1900, Prof Joly wrote to Mr Proud:
The telephone has been put up for some time but I understand it will not be ready for use until the rent has been paid. However, before paying the rent, I shall be obliged if you will insist on the alteration of the position of one of the poles here. It was put up without my knowledge in a most objectionable position. I wrote to the manager requesting alteration but have received no reply.

On 22 March, G.W. Gwyther wrote to Mr Proud:
I am in receipt of your letter of 19th inst, re pole erected on Dunsink route. This will be shifted at the earliest possible moment and I regret that Prof. Joly objects to it.

On 10 April 1900, G.W. Gwyther wrote to Mr Proud:
I am in receipt of your letter of the 9th inst, enclosing copy of letter received by you from the Astronomer. I would point out that the delay in joining up this wire is due to our not receiving a reply to our letter of 8th ult asking for cheque for rental.

On 18 April, G.W. Gwyther wrote to Mr Proud:

> I am in receipt of your letter of the 17th inst and beg to inform you that the delay in connecting your wire is due to the fact that we have not yet received cheque for rent of same. The pole referred to has nothing to do with it and will be attended to at the earliest possible moment.

On 20 April 1900, Professor Joly wrote to Mr Proud:

> I enclose letter from the Manager of the Telephone Company stating that the delay in connecting the wire is because he has not received the rent. The pole has not yet been shifted. It would much facilitate matters in getting your clock right if we could use the telephone.

As there is no further correspondence in the archive concerning the telephone, it is assumed that Castleknock 14 came into use by the end of April 1900, three years after it was first suggested by Professor Rambaut.

3.11 Further Problems

Despite improvements made to the time service by Ball and Rambaut, Professor Joly's tenure at Dunsink was not free of problems. Surprisingly, these involved mostly the precision Dent clock in the Ballast Office boardroom, which started to behave irregularly from October 1899 and even stopped. It was thought at first that the clock needed to be cleaned and this was done by Messrs Frengley of 5 Crow Street at a cost of £3-5-0 in December. However, the trouble continued and Charles Longford reported on 8 January 1900 that the Dent clock had stopped again. He also pointed out that the minute hand of the 'Front' clock was travelling ahead of the second hand. The problems of the Dent clock continued into March and affected the dropping of the time ball. Yeates were consulted and at first they declared that it was in perfect working order, but later admitted that there was a fault with the pendulum magnets.

> By 28 March 1900, a tone of frustration had crept into Mr Longford's reports to Professor Joly:
> Since Thursday 8th inst the Board Clock has been going wrong each day. I examine the Clock each morning between 9.30 and 10.00 a.m. and then correct errors putting everything right, never neglecting to do so. You will be able to satisfy yourself about this in Dunsink any morning. Yeates says the Board Clock is in perfect order but since then one morning I find the clock has gained several seconds in the preceding 24 hours, and that on the next morning I find the clock to have lost several seconds I fail to see where the perfect order comes in. Also the errors are quite different each morning sometimes 15 or 20 seconds difference. …

This led Professor Joly to write to Mr Proud on 30 March:

> I received your letter this morning and the copy of Messrs Yeates singularly contradictory letter in which they state they 'are sorry to learn that the Board Room Clock has been going irregularly and the Time Ball falling late' and yet they 'beg to assume that the clock and its connections are in perfect order and adjustment'.
>
> The question remains now what do you propose doing under the circumstances? The repeated irregularity will throw discredit on the Time Service and most unjustly

for there are few observations in which greater accuracy is maintained. If Messrs Yeates are unable or unwilling to put the clock in proper order and if no other firm be got to do it, the only course open to me is to publish full particulars of the irregularities in order to exonerate myself and my assistant.

By the end of April, the board had instructed Yeates to overhaul the Dent clock and, while they were doing that, they could include a 'drop second' arrangement to report the state of the clock to Dunsink as suggested by Professor Joly. Yeates questioned the need for the drop second and claimed it would need 'very careful handling and skilled attention'.

On 12 May, Professor Joly wrote to Mr Proud:

My statements in my letter of 7th inst which Yeates contradicts are completely verified by reference to the daily records in the Observatory clock book. I have looked back in this book to the 1st of January last year. I find on every occasion on which the Trinity clock went wrong with one solitary exception Yeates delayed to set it right until the following Monday, the day on which the clock is wound, although he had received timely warning from me by telegram or by letter or messenger. The single exception occurred on the 9th inst. The clock went astray because Yeates disconnected your wires on the 7th and did not make the connection good. On account of his systematic delay in setting the Trinity College Clock right after any accidental interruption of the current, I have been on the point of making a formal complaint to the Board of TCD time after time. You may not be aware that Yeates has a contract for keeping this clock right. It thus appears that even when the Trinity clock is wrong Yeates does not pay any attention to it until the day for winding, and I should be greatly surprised if he paid any attention to it except on that day when the clock is going right.

As Yeates has on this occasion and privately made statements that have every appearance of being inaccurate and misleading I shall not reply in detail to his letters in future. I have given my opinion that the 'drop second' apparatus will give no trouble if properly fitted and I am more than ever convinced of the truth of this statement. Of course I merely offered you this suggestion in the hope of improving the Time Service. It is no concern of mine what arrangements you make about your clocks. I shall be however always happy to offer you any suggestions I think may be useful.

Yeates completed their overhaul of the clocks on 12 September and gave a report of the work they had done. They traced the problems to the current supply, which had been increased by the Post Office, probably to counteract interference from the electric trams, which were then replacing the horse-drawn trams. Yeates fitted a new controlling coil to the Dent clock and, after some adjustment, got the clock under proper control. They also fitted new controlling coils to the TCD clock and the Ballast Office 'Front' clock resulting in similar improvements.

3.12 Exit Yeates & Son

On 4 February 1901, Yeates wrote to Mr Proud:

We regret to inform you that we are no longer in a position to repair or adjust the clocks or time signalling apparatus. Should any further repairs or adjustments be

3.22—Electric-powered trams in Westmoreland Street. CREATIVE COMMONS

Westmoreland Street, Dublin   *Showing Sackville St. in distance*

necessary, Messrs Frengley of Crow Street who have charge of several systems of electric clocks, would, we believe, be willing to undertake them.

On 10 September 1901, Mr Proud gave the following summary to the Port and Docks Board: The Clock outside building is controlled from Dunsink Observatory. The Astronomer Royal [sic] undertakes onerous duties to give correct time by it to the citizens, and Time Ball on the roof is electrically dropped daily by him at 1 O'C. Greenwich. In 1899 [actually April 1900] telephonic communication was established to the Observatory to facilitate the supervision and to at once put right any faults, for which the Board pay £11 annually. On 6th June 1901, the services of the Astronomer's Assistant (Mr Longford) for superintending the clocks &c. at a payment of £12 per annum, were dispensed with, but he was reappointed from same date at a yearly payment of £2 [i.e. 1.3 pence per day!] 'for daily correcting errors and for winding the Ballast Office Clocks which are connected electrically with Dunsink Observatory'. Messrs Frengley look after the Board Room annual Clock for which they have been paid £3-5s annually since they cleaned it in December 1899. Messrs Chancellor wind the new clock in the Board Room erected by them.

In July 1902, Frengley Brothers were asked to quote for renovating the time ball. They reported: … we have made a thorough examination of the same and find it is in a very bad condition. It is made of light wood, covered with canvas which has become rotten at the bottom and some of the stays have also given way.

They gave an estimate for recovering the 4-foot diameter ball with canvas and repainting it for £ 10-15-0.

The year 1905 was a fateful one for Professor Joly. During the year he had visited South Africa with the British Association. Shortly after his return, his young daughter Jessie contracted typhoid. After he became ill he wrote to a friend: 'If the attack is as severe as little Jessie's I know quite well I cannot hold out. For myself I am content though I confess I should like to be allowed to finish my life's work'. Jessie recovered but Joly died on 4 January 1906 at the age of only 41, probably due to contamination of the Observatory's water supply.

3.13 Edmund Taylor Whittaker: 7th Royal Astronomer

The next Andrews Professor was Edmund Taylor Whittaker, Fellow of Trinity College, Cambridge, who took up residence at Dunsink in June 1906 at the age of 33. Although the research work of the Observatory was now mainly concerned with astronomical photography, Mr Charles Martin continued the transit observations and maintained the time service.

During April 1910, the Dunsink line was being interrupted frequently causing disruption of the time service. As his letters to the Post Office were being ignored, Professor Whittaker wrote a strongly worded letter to the Port and Docks Board on 20 April:

> … The purpose of the present letter is to call the attention of the Port and Docks Board to the fact that the wire is as a matter of fact frequently interrupted (presumably by the Post Office Telegraph engineer but as to that I have no information); and that in consequence the Ballast Office clock is frequently in discord with the Dunsink clock. … The Port and Docks Board will of course decide for themselves what course to adopt under the circumstances; but I hope I may be permitted to express the opinion that no attempt at reform can be satisfactory which does not provide for a strict formal guarantee from the officials of the Post Office Telegraphs that the wire connecting Dunsink to the Ballast Office shall not be interrupted at any time under any circumstances, except when it is actually in disrepair.

The trouble must have continued as the secretary of the GPO in Dublin wrote to Mr Proud on 14 June:

> In reply to your letter of 2nd ultimo respecting the faulty working of the wire between Dunsink Observatory and the Port & Docks Office, I have to inform you that only two causes for recent irregularity are recorded, viz a breakage of the wire during the snowstorm at the end of January and a similar breakage on the 18th April. The line has been carefully examined and is reported to be in good order at present. The inconvenience occasioned by the interruptions of the circuit is regretted and I should be glad if, in the event of any irregularity occurring in future, you would be good enough to communicate immediately with the Post Office Superintending Engineer, Aldborough House, Dublin (Telephone, Post Office Dublin 36) in order that prompt attention may be given to the matter.

There is no further correspondence on the matter.

Professor Whittaker left Dunsink in 1912 to become professor of Mathematics in the University of Edinburgh.

3.23—O'Connell Street in the aftermath of the 1916 Rising. The front clock of the Ballast Office continued to operate despite the shelling. KEOGH BROTHERS, WIKIMEDIA COMMONS

3.14 Henry Crozier Plummer: 8th Royal Astronomer

Whittaker was succeeded by Henry Crozier Plummer who became the 8th Royal Astronomer.

3.15 Charles Richard Longford

On 4 May 1916, Mr Longford wrote to Mr Proud:

> The Front Street Clock continued to work all through the past troublesome times [The Easter Rising, 24-29 April], but as we have no wire connection with Dunsink Observatory, I cannot guarantee the time showing is correct or not. If you desire, I shall cycle out to the Observatory and bring in the correct time but I must first get a pass out of the City. I cannot get one myself and so apply to you for further instructions.

On 28 October 1930, Mr Longford wrote to Mr Proud:

> When Sir Robert Ball was appointed Lowndean Astronomer at Cambridge University in 1892 resigning Dunsink, he recommended me as successor to his son to the Ballast Office Clocks connected with Dunsink at £12 per annum. Later on my brother-in-law Prof. Rambaut was appointed to Oxford University about 1900 and Mr Proud reduced this to £4 per annum. Now times are very much changed since that date, and living expenses in the Free State are very high and increasing constantly. I would ask if I could possibly have this £4 increased. I may add that during the time (about 37 years) I have always regularly and faithfully attended to the duties connected to the Clocks.

Mr Longford's salary was increased to £10 from 1 July 1931.

The last letter from this conscientious man is dated 17 July 1935, aged 68 and 43 years after he was engaged by Arthur Rambaut. He wrote to the secretary, Mr E.H. Bailey, from the Old Men's Home, Leeson Park:

> I want to thank you for all you have so kindly done for me. I am very comfortable here and everybody is very kind to me. I am afraid I will not be able to attend any longer to the Ballast Office Clocks, and beg to resign my position.

Charles Richard Longford never married. He lived in lodgings in Ranelagh and Clontarf before moving to 126 North Strand, Fairview, about 1901–07 where he lived alone. In the 1911 Census he described his occupation as Dentistry and Dental Anaesthetist. By the time of his retirement, he was described as being 'painfully deaf'. He died on 30 December1939 aged 73.

3.16 The Death of Nicholas Proud

On 13 March 1921, Nicholas Proud died at his home, 77 Pembroke Road. He had served the Port and Docks Board for 59 years, the last 54 as an efficient and conscientious secretary and he had dealt with all the trials and tribulations of the time service. It was his custom to always wind the Dent 12-month clock on New Year Day. He was succeeded by Edward H. Bailey.

He achieved a measure of immortality by being mentioned in Chapter 1.1 of James Joyce's *Finnegans Wake,* published in 1939:

> Stand up mickos! Make strake for sinners! By order Nicholas Proud.

One commentator identifies Proud with the devil on the grounds that Irenaeus said Satan fell because of pride and arrogance and envy of God's creation.

In 1960, the Port and Docks Board sold the Ballast Office premises on Westmoreland Street and, after being accommodated temporarily for some years, moved in 1981 to the Dublin Port Centre on Alexandra Road. The Dent clocks were moved to the foyer of the Centre and they still keep excellent time. The famous Ballast Office Clock was moved to the Aston Quay façade of the Royal Liver Assurance building and continues to provide Dubliners with the 'right time'.

4. Ulysses and the end of Dublin Time

Timeball on the ballastoffice is down. Dunsink time.
Leopold Bloom in *Ulysses* by James Joyce

4.1 Joyce and the Time Ball

While the Ballast Office time ball and the Watch Tower have faded into oblivion, the time ball itself has gained a measure of immortality by its mention in James Joyce's *Ulysses*. As the events of Bloomsday on 16 June 1904 unfold, there are a number of references to the ball, the time service and Dunsink Observatory.

4.01—James Joyce, author of *Ulysses* and creator of the character Leopold Bloom, in 1934 . Jacques-Émile Blanche, NGI, Creative Commons

As Leopold Bloom wanders from Sackville Street (now O'Connell Street) towards Davy Byrne's pub he notices that the time ball on the Ballast Office roof is down and assumes it must be after 1 p.m. and he mentions 'Dunsink Time'. However, while the Ballast Office Clock would have been showing Dublin Time as defined by the longitude of Dunsink, in 1904 the time ball was being released at 1 p.m. Greenwich Time.

4.02—A drawing by James Joyce of his character. Leopold Bloom, or Poldy.

Mr Bloom moved forward, raising his troubled eyes. Think no more about that. After one. Timeball on the ballastoffice is down. Dunsink time. Fascinating little book that is of sir Robert Ball's. Parallax. I never exactly understood. There's a priest. Could ask him. Par it's Greek: parallel, parallax [para Gr. beside].

He muses on the term 'parallax' and remembers Robert Ball's explanation of parallax in *The Story of the Heavens* which he had in his library:

> We must first explain clearly the conception which is known to astronomers by the name of parallax; for it is by parallax that the distance of the Sun, or, indeed, the distance of any other celestial body, must be determined. Let us take a simple illustration. Stand near a window whence you can look at buildings, or the trees, the clouds, or any distant objects. Place on the glass a thin strip of paper vertically in the middle of one of the panes. Close the right eye, and note with the left eye the position of the strip of paper relatively to the objects in the background. Then, while still remaining in the same position, close the left eye and again observe the position of the strip of paper with the right eye. You will find that the position of the paper on the background has changed. As I sit in my study and look out of the window I see a strip of paper, with my right eye, in front of a certain bough on a tree a couple of hundred yards away; with my left eye the paper is no longer in front of that bough, it has moved to a position near the outline of the tree. This apparent displacement of the strip of paper, relatively to the distant background, is what is called parallax.

'It is this principle,' Ball points out, 'applied on a gigantic scale, which enables us to measure the distances of the heavenly bodies'.

4.2 An Encounter with Endymion

Bloom meets an old friend, Mrs Breen, and they notice one of Dublin's characters approaching. It is 'Endymion', otherwise known as Cashel Boyle O'Connor Fitzmaurice Tisdall Farrell, who haunted Grafton Street and College Green.

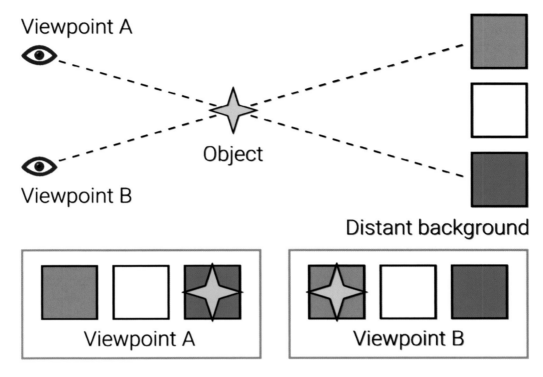

4.03—Diagram of the perspective change in a parallax. Viewed from point A the yellow star appears to be in front of the blue square; from viewpoint B, it appears to have moved to in front of the red square. JUSTIN WICK, ENGLISH WIKIPEDIA, CREATIVE COMMONS 3.0.

He wore a deerstalker hat, knee breeches, tunic shirt and buckled shoes. He carried a few swords, a fishing rod and an umbrella which was raised on a fine day and down on a wet day. He always gave a sword salute to the Ballast Office clock and set his alarm clock by it. He would wet his finger and hold it up to see which way the wind was blowing; then taking a compass bearing he would head for home.

Mr Bloom touched her funnybone gently, warning her. – Mind! Let this man pass. A bony form strode along the curbstone from the river, staring with a rapt gaze into the sunlight through a heavy stringed glass. Tight as a skullpiece a tiny hat gripped his head. From his arm a folded dustcoat, a stick and an umbrella dangled to his stride.
— Watch him, Mr Bloom said. He always walks outside the lampposts. Watch!
— Who is he if it's a fair question, Mrs Breen asked. Is he dotty?
— His name is Cashel Boyle O'Connor Fitzmaurice Tisdall Farrell, Mr Bloom said, smiling. Watch!
— He has enough of them, she said. Denis [her husband] will be like that one of these days.
She broke off suddenly.
— There he is, she said. I must go after him. Goodbye. Remember me to Molly, won't you?
— I will, Mr Bloom said.

4.3 An Optical Interlude

Bloom moves on towards Grafton Street and stops at No. 2 on the corner to look at the field glasses in the optician's window.

> He crossed at Nassau street corner and stood before the window of Yeates and Son pricing the fieldglasses. Or will I drop into old Harris's and have a chat with young Sinclair? Wellmannered fellow. Probably at his lunch. Must get those old glasses of mine set right. Goerz lenses six guineas. … There's a little watch up there on the roof of the bank to test those glasses by. His lids came down on the lower rims of his irides [plural of iris]. Can't see it. If you imagine it's there you can almost see it. Can't see it

Viewing a watch face is a common way of testing a telescope or a pair of binoculars but it is not surprising that Bloom can't see the tiny watch face on the roof of the bank building.

> He faced about and, standing between the awnings, held out his right hand at arm's length towards the sun. Wanted to try that often. Yes: completely. The tip of his little finger blotted out the sun's disk. Must be the focus where the rays cross. If I had black glasses. Interesting. There was a lot of talk about those sunspots when we were in Lombard street west. Looking up from the back garden. Terrific explosions they are. There will be a total eclipse this year: autumn some time.

It is remarkable that the method used by Bloom for looking at the sun is exactly that used by professional astronomers for estimating the clarity of the sky when observing the corona. However,

4.04—The premises of Yeates & Son, Grafton Street, Dublin.

his mention of 'black glasses' is unfortunate as using darkened glass can be a harmful way of looking at the solar disk. Projecting an image is safer. The number of spots on the sun was a maximum in 1897 and a minimum in 1904. The total solar eclipse occurred on 9 September 1904 but the path of totality lay across an uninhabited part of the Pacific Ocean.

4.4 Joyce and Dunsink Observatory

Now that I come to think of it that ball falls at Greenwich time. It's the clock is worked by an electric wire from Dunsink. Must go out there some first Saturday of the month. If I could get an introduction to professor Joly or learn up something about his family. That would do to: man always feels complimented. Flattery where least expected. Nobleman proud to be descended from some king's mistress. His foremother. Lay it on with a trowel. Cap in hand goes through the land. Not go in and blurt out what you know you're not to: what's parallax? Show this gentleman the door.

Bloom has second thoughts about the actual time the ball indicates. Joyce must have been aware that the fall of the ball was at 1 p.m. GMT in 1904 and Dubliners who wished to set their watches by Greenwich Time would look out for its release. Joyce knew that the Observatory welcomed visitors on the first Saturday of the month. The admission card signed by Arthur Rambaut advises walkers to follow the 'single Telegraph Wire' to the Observatory; this wire carried the signals for the time ball.

Bloom next ponders what he knows about stars and how they evolve. Such knowledge was still very incomplete at the beginning of the twentieth century. New Moon had occurred on 13 June so it was only three days old on the 16th.

4.05—Admission card to Dunsink Observatory.

ADMISSION TO DUNSINK OBSERVATORY.

The Assistant Astronomer will show the Observatory to Visitors on the first Saturday in each month, from 3 to 5 o'Clock in the afternoon, and in the evening, from 7 to 9 o'Clock, p.m., during the Winter half of the year (from October   March inclusive), and from 9 to 11 p.m. during the other months.

ROUTE FOR DRIVING.

Up Cabra Road to where four roads meet.   Take the road to the right, passing the entrance to the large School on the left, and on straight to the Railway Crossing ; thence follow a single Telegraph Wire.

ROUTE FOR WALKING.

Up the Banks of the Royal Canal, to where a single Telegraph Wire diverges to a road on the right.   Follow that Wire.

ARTHUR A. RAMBAUT,
Royal Astronomer of Ireland.

Never know anything about it. Waste of time. Gasballs spinning about, crossing each other, passing. Same old dingdong always. Gas: then solid: then world: then cold: then dead shell drifting around, frozen rock, like that pineapple rock. The moon. Must be anew moon out, she said. I believe there is.

In the next extract Joyce confuses Dunsink with the seismological observatory at Rathfarnham that was run by Father William O'Leary, S.J. (1869–1939). O'Leary installed the first Irish seismograph, of his own design, at Mungret College, Limerick, in 1908. In 1916, it was moved to Rathfarnham Castle where it was in operation until 1961. The reference to an earthquake in 1534 may be based on a paper *An Essay on the Climate of Ireland*, which Dr Joseph McSweeny read to the Royal Irish Academy on 8 November 1830; it contains the entry: '1584 An earthquake happened at Dublin, which accident is so rare in Ireland, that when it falls out so, it is esteemed a prodigy'.

The catastrophe was terrific and instantaneous in its effect. The observatory of Dunsink registered in all eleven shocks, all of the fifth grade of Mercalli's scale, and there is no record extant of a similar seismic disturbance in our island since the earthquake of 1534, the year of the rebellion of Silken Thomas.

Bloom then daydreams about attending a reception at the Viceregal Lodge in the Phoenix Park and indulges in a bit of name dropping:

BLOOM: (IN COURT DRESS) Can give best references. Messrs Callan, Coleman.

4.06—Rathfarnham Castle in 1899. FLICKR COMMONS

Mr Wisdom Hely J. P. My old chief Joe Cuffe. Mr V. B. Dillon, ex lord mayor of Dublin.
I have moved in the charmed circle of the highest ... Queens of Dublin society.
(CARELESSLY) I was just chatting this afternoon at the viceregal lodge to my old
pals, sir Robert and lady Ball, astronomer royal at the levee. Sir Bob, I said ...

Later, Lenehan and McCoy see Bloom buying a book and mention his preference for
astronomical books:

They went up the steps and under Merchants' arch. A darkbacked figure scanned books
on the hawker's cart.
—There he is, Lenehan said.
—Wonder what he's buying, M'Coy said, glancing behind.
—Leopoldo or the Bloom is on the Rye, Lenehan said.
—He's dead nuts on sales, M'Coy said. I was with him one day and he bought a book
from an old one in Liffey street for two bob. There were fine plates in it worth double
the money, the stars and the moon and comets with long tails. Astronomy it was about.

These extracts show well how Joyce used actual places and events as a framework for his great
work that continues to fascinate or frustrate its readers. Some commentators have claimed that Joyce's
later works were influenced by Einstein's Special Theory of Relativity of 1905 and his General
Theory of 1915. This may be true for *Finnegan's Wake*, which was written between 1922 and 1939
but it is less likely for Ulysses, which was written between 1914 and 1922. Nevertheless, his habit of
switching between two different viewpoints may have its origin in the astronomical concept of
parallax.

4.5 The Royal Dublin Society Time Service

In April 1873, the council of the Royal Dublin Society (RDS) requested its Committee of Science to report on the feasibility of setting up a time service for Dublin. On 5 August, three committee members, G. Johnstone Stoney, Howard Grubb and Robert Ball (then Professor of Mechanics at the Royal College of Science), compared a pocket chronometer with the clocks at the stations along the Dublin–Kingstown railway line, with public clocks and with the clocks of some clockmakers. They were rather dismayed at the large range of errors they observed. The largest discrepancy was at the Alliance Gas Company where the clock was seven minutes 13 seconds fast compared to the mean. The General Post Office and two clockmakers were just 13 seconds fast on the mean and that was probably the correct time to a second or so. The worst railway clock was at Sydney Parade Station where the error was three minutes fast.

The members of the sub-committee recommended the best method for controlling a number of clocks. They described the system that had operated in Liverpool for 17 years and in Edinburgh for 12 years. The idea of a Scottish clockmaker, Alexander Bain (1811–1877), for sympathetic pendulums was improved and patented in 1857 by R.L. Jones, a Chester stationmaster. A good quality clock (the master) was compared every day with a telegraphed signal from Greenwich.

4.08—A view of the Dublin to Kingstown railway line at Seapoint in 1834. CREATIVE COMMONS

4.09—The physicist George Johnstone Stoney in the 1890s. CREATIVE COMMONS

4.6 Operating Principle of Ritchie Master and Slave System

4.10—Frederick James Ritchie of the Scottish clockmaking firm James Ritchie & Son.

In 1872, James Ritchie improved Bain's system. The diagram shows on the right the slave clock with its pendulum coil passing over two permanent magnets with unlike poles facing each other. On the left, the pendulum of the master clock closes contacts at the extremities of each swing and energises the coil of the slave pendulum, keeping it in step with the master. The energised coil of the slave is equivalent to a magnet with alternating polarity. The contacts are connected to the positive and negative terminals of a Daniell 10-cell battery with its centre point earthed. The master clock and a number of slave clocks are connected in series and each clock has a tell-tale indicator that shows the flow of the electrical pulses and their polarity. A fine example of a Ritchie slave clock is shown in picture 4.12.

The committee estimated the cost of providing a time service for Dublin. A good quality clock to serve as master would cost from £40 to £70 and slave clocks of sufficient quality would cost £8 to £11 each. The telegraph wire would be installed by the Post Office for an annual rent of £7 per mile and the Greenwich signal would be £17 p.a. Taking all expenses into account, a

4.11—Diagram showing the working of Ritchie master and slave pendulum clocks.

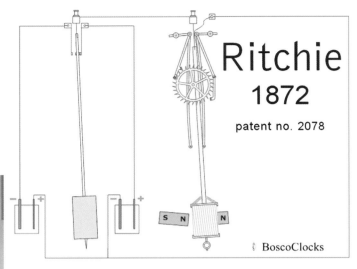

4.12 (left)—A Ritchie slave clock.

4.13 (below)—The Royal Dublin Society Ritchie master clock used for the provision of a time service for Dublin.

system consisting of a master clock and 20 slaves would cost £132 per annum.

The recommendations of the sub-committee were adopted and in November 1873 the RDS placed an order for a Ritchie master clock costing £66 and a slave clock costing £14-5-0. Thirty-eight commercial firms and institutions expressed interest in using the service at an annual cost of £6-12-0 per clock. Each day at 10 a.m. GMT, i.e., 9.35 a.m. Dublin Time, a telegraph signal was received via the GPO and the master clock was checked. The system came into use in November 1874 and operated for about 25 years under the direction of a Time Control Committee. From January 1876, Yeates and Son were responsible for the maintenance of the system for £60 per annum. The system was abandoned about 1891 because the growth in telegraph and telephone traffic caused inductive coupling between adjacent wires and the resulting interference rendered the clock signals unreliable.

4.14—The RDS slave clock.

4.7 Local Solar Time Gives Way to Mean Time

In Britain the growth of the railways led to the abandonment of Local Mean Time and the introduction of London Time (GMT). The Great Western Railway was the first to adopt London Time in November 1840. Other railways followed suit and by 1848 most stations used GMT. By 1855, most public clocks in Britain were set to GMT but some were fitted with two minute hands, one for local time and the other for GMT.

On one of his forays into the Irish countryside, John Pentland Mahaffy (1839–1919), the distinguished Provost of Trinity, missed a train because the time on the clock outside the station differed from that on the clock inside. When he took one of the locals to task for this affront to his efficiency, he received the answer: 'if they told the same time, they'd be no need to have two clocks'.

In 1880, Parliament passed an Act defining legal time in Great Britain to be Greenwich Mean Time and in Ireland, Dublin Mean Time. Unfortunately, 'Dublin Time' was not defined explicitly, which led to some confusion. Dublin Time was defined in the Nautical Almanac by reference to the meridian through the transit instrument in Dunsink, which Revd Dr. John Brinkley had estimated in 1832 to be 0h 25m 22s west of Greenwich; this value was changed to Robinson's estimate of 0h 25m 21.1s about 1896. On the other hand, Leinster House was less than a second of time from the 25-minute meridian so that the 10 a.m. signal from Greenwich arrived at Leinster House at 9.35 a.m. local mean time. However, Professor Ball was a member of the RDS Time Control Committee and no doubt he would have insisted that Dublin Time was in fact Dunsink Time.

On 17 February 1885, W.W. Kindle of the Board of Trade again wrote to the Port and Docks Board pointing out that the time ball fell not in

4.15—John Pentland Mahaffy, Provost of Trinity College Dublin.

accordance with the local time of its longitude but at a time related to the longitude of Dunsink, which he gave as 19 seconds of time (or 4' 45" of longitude) in error. In view of the adoption of Greenwich as the prime meridian, he thought it would be advantageous for the Dublin time ball to be connected to Greenwich. Copies of his letter were sent to the Harbour Master and to Professor Ball. The former supported the dropping of the time ball at noon GMT. Professor Ball, in a letter dated 5 February, stated that 'the time of Ireland has always been understood as the time of Dunsink and the mariner who refers to the Nautical Almanac can hardly be led astray as the longitude of Dublin there given is the longitude of Dunsink'. He pointed out that considerable confusion would be caused in making a change and that he would prefer to see GMT used throughout Ireland but that the control of the time ball and the Port and Docks clock should remain with Dunsink. He would like to have the time ball dropped at 1 p.m. GMT instead of 1 p.m. Dublin Time. The TCD board, however, thought that 'a great inconvenience would be caused by dropping the time ball at 12h 34m 38s local time instead of at present 13 o'clock'. They were recognising the public's habit when passing over Carlisle (O'Connell) Bridge at 1 p.m. of checking their watches by the fall of the time ball. There is no evidence from the records that Professor Ball got his wish to have the time ball dropped at 1 p.m. GMT but by 1899 those Dubliners who used Greenwich Time were accustomed to set their watches by the fall of the ball.

In January 1909, *The Irish Times* reported that the Dublin Chamber of Commerce had passed unanimously a resolution: 'That the Government be requested to extend Greenwich Time to Ireland and thereby render the clock time of the British Isles uniform'. An article in the *Horological Journal* for September 1911 pointed out that all the Irish Chambers of Commerce were agreed on the adoption of Greenwich Time for Ireland. Nevertheless, there were conservatives such as Mr William

4.16—The time ball on the Ballast Office roof.

Field M.P. of Blackrock, Co. Dublin, who was a member of the board and who thought the proposal 'as being opposed to the natural law and general usage of Ports'.

4.8 Summer Time Introduced and the End of Dublin Mean Time

Summer Time was first introduced into the United Kingdom in May 1916 as a result of a vigorous campaign led by William Willet, an English builder. Despite the protests of farmers, clocks were put forward by one hour from 2.00 a.m. on Sunday, 20 May 1916. This meant the adjustment of the Ballast Office Clock and all other public clocks in Dublin.

The time difference between Ireland and Britain was found inconvenient for telegraphic communication and the Time (Ireland) Act, 1916 provided that Ireland would adopt Greenwich Mean Time from 2:00 a.m. Dublin Mean Time on Sunday, 1 October 1916; this also coincided with the end of Summer Time. It was ironic that the year of the Rising brought dependence on Greenwich Time and united the two islands in a common time zone.

After 1916, depending on where you were, clocks could show four possible times: Dunsink, Greenwich and the summer variations on either, with a maximum difference of one hour and 25 minutes. Even four years later, in 1920, when the IRA activist, Ernie O'Malley, was a training officer for IRA units there was still considerable confusion about what time it was. O'Malley wrote in his memoir of the period:

> There was the difficulty of [having] three different times for councils and classes.
> Summer time was kept by cities, some towns and the railway; new time was an increase

4.17—The path of the
international prime
meridian at the Royal
Observatory Greenwich.
HANS BÉZARD, CREATIVE
COMMONS 4.0

of 25 minutes on old Irish [Dublin] time to synchronise with English time; as yet
punctual time had not yet come.

In September 1919, Mr F.A. Campion, Chief Engineer of the Great Northern Railway Company,
wrote to the Port and Docks Board to see if the 1 p.m. signal could be sent to a master clock to be
installed in Amiens Street Station, Dublin. The matter was referred to Joseph Mallagh, the Chief
Engineer to the board. Mr Mallagh pointed out that the new arrangement would require the wire
from Dunsink to the Ballast Office to fan out to Trinity College, the time ball at the Watch House
on the South Wall, the RDS premises in Kildare Street and the GNR Station in Amiens Street. In
view of increased Post Office charges, he suggested the RDS and the GNR should each pay one
third of the annual rental of the Dunsink line plus a two-guinea annual connection fee. The RDS
decided to discontinue the arrangement but thanked the board and its officials for 'the courteous
manner in which the requirements of the Society were attended to in the long period [from 1893]
during which the Society obtained correct time through the Board's offices'. The Amiens Street
station was connected to the Dunsink circuit in February 1921 but the link was terminated only
four years later, in February 1925.

4.9 A Proposal for a Clock Tower on the South Wall
In February 1906, John P. Griffith, the port Chief Engineer, proposed that a brick Watch House be
constructed at the end of the South Wall to replace a temporary wooden hut then used by the
Harbour Master's men when on duty there. It was designed so that it could be raised to form a clock
tower, which some people thought was greatly needed in the port.

The Watch House was also known as the 'Hailing Station', the name being derived from the custom in the nineteenth century of a ship's master hailing the station on arrival to give details of the vessel, its cargo, etc.; conversely, the master would be told the berth he was to take. Later, with the growth of the docks to the east, a new hailing station was built at the Eastern Breakwater in 1953.

With the closing of Butt Bridge to shipping in December 1888 and with the completion of the Loopline railway bridge in 1891, shipping was confined to the river east of Butt Bridge and mariners had not a good sight of the time ball on the corner of the Ballast Office. In 1908, the Port and Docks Board considered a proposal to erect a public clock at the east end of Sir John Rogerson's Quay and also move the time ball there. The plan was to erect a tower on the existing Watch House and to display the time with four six-foot illuminated dials. The Chief Engineer gave a preliminary estimate of £350 for the tower and the clock mechanism. Sir Howard Grubb of the famous telescope firm was consulted and gave an estimate of £200 for a clock system similar to that used for driving equatorial telescopes so that the equatorial axis of the Earth is synchronised with the perpendicular axis of the sky. A revised estimate for building the tower amounted to £216. The board considered the proposal and resolved: 'That in the present demands on the funds of the port it is inexpedient to proceed at present with the clock and that the matter be postponed for six months'. A further two postponements took place and there was no more discussion of the proposal.

4.10 The Time Ball is Moved to the South Wall

The matter of the unseeable time ball came to a head in October 1915 when the Harbour Master of Dublin port wrote to the Port and Docks Board pointing out that mariners were unable to regulate their chronometers. As the existing time ball was in a state of decay, Mr Griffith proposed that it be rebuilt by his department and erected at the Watch House; this was achieved by the beginning of April 1916. The Post Office charged £2-12-6 for extending the telegraph line to the Watch House.

"TIME BALL" UNNECESSARY

The hailing station at the South Wall, showing the "time ball," used for signalling the correct time to mariners. The ball is to be removed, as it was damaging the roof and had become unnecessary.

4.19—A newspaper report about the planned removal of the time ball from the Watch House roof in 1948.

4.11 The Last Years of the Time Ball

From August 1937, a temporary radio receiver was installed at the Ballast Office to receive international time signals so that the local clock could be kept nearly correct to control the front street clock of the Ballast Office and to regulate the fall of the time ball on Sir John Rogerson's Quay.

Professor J.J. Dowling of University College devised a permanent system to receive the time signal from the radio station operated by the UK Post Office at Rugby in Warwickshire and to control the fall of the time ball. His system had a variation of less than one-fifth of a second per week and came into operation in March 1940.

On 20 May 1948, the Harbour Master wrote to Mr R.F. Lowe who was the secretary to the Port and Docks Board:

> During the last few years it has been increasingly difficult to make the roof of the Hailing Station watertight, and the Engineer informs me that this is due to the fact that the existing Time Ball is shaking the building every time it drops. In order to make the roof watertight, it would be necessary to spend a considerable amount of money, to prevent the fall of the Time Ball damaging the roof.
>
> I am of the opinion that the Time Ball is never used by vessels coming to the Port of Dublin, in view of the fact that practically all vessels which require time signals for

4.20—Prof. Hermann A. Brück who had the time ball taken to Dunsink Observatory.

checking their chronometers are fitted with radio telegraphy and can check their chronometers by radio time signals. In view of this fact I think that the Time Ball should be removed, but I presume that before doing so that the Department of Industry and Commerce should be informed.

The department had no objection to the removal of the time ball and it was taken down later that year and given to Dunsink Observatory. Professor Hermann A. Brück, the new Director of the Observatory under the Dublin Institute for Advanced Studies, had suggested that the ball might be re-mounted in the grounds of Dunsink near the transit circle. The ball was delivered to Dunsink but was never set up again and gradually disintegrated in an outhouse.

The Watch House itself survived into the 21st century but in a very dilapidated state. In 2006, the Dublin Docklands Development Authority commissioned a conservation report on the listed building and the consultants recommended 'conservation by record'. The demolition of the Watch House early one morning in August 2007 provoked some critical comment in the newspapers.

5. Dunsink Observatory and its astronomers

I ofen looked up at the sky an' assed meself the question - what is the moon, what is the stars?
Captain Boyle, Act I, *Juno and the Paycock* by Sean O'Casey (1880–1964)

5.1 The Science of Astronomy

There is a common perception that astronomy is a very esoteric science dealing with stars and galaxies at unimaginable distances and with little relevance to everyday life. However, the reality is quite different as astronomy has its origin in very practical affairs.

The first astronomers were preoccupied with tracking the seasons as the spinning Earth circles the Sun and they reconciled the natural cycles of year, month and day to produce a variety of calendars. The Sumerian year had 12 months of 29 or 30 days but lacked weeks. The Mayans used two separate years – the 260-day Sacred Round and the 365-day Vague Year – which combined to form a 52-year cycle. The Athenians had a luni–solar calendar lasting 364 days with an intercalary month added every year. The Vikings had only two seasons: summer and winter. The discordance in the lengths of the day and the year were eventually reconciled in the West by the introduction of the Gregorian calendar in 1582; the purpose of the reformers was to keep the vernal equinox on much the same date.

One of the first modern observatories to be established was the Paris Observatory, founded by Louis XIV in 1667 on the advice of his minister Jean-Baptiste Colbert who wished to strengthen France's maritime power and promote its international trade. The world's first national almanac, the *Connaissance des temps,* was published by the observatory in 1679, using eclipses in Jupiter's satellites to aid seafarers in establishing longitude.

The Royal Greenwich Observatory (RGO) in London was established in 1675 by Charles II and the position of Astronomer Royal was created to direct the observatory and to:
apply himself with the most exact care and diligence to the rectifying of the table of the motions of the heavens, and the places of the fixed stars, so as to find out the so much desired longitude of places for perfecting the art of navigation.

In essence, Britain was a seafaring nation and its mariners needed to be able to navigate the oceans with confidence and in safety. The RGO published the first *Nautical Almanac and Astronomical Ephemeris* in 1767 and it became every navigator's bible. The close link between the RGO and the Admiralty continued right up to 1965 when the Observatory was placed under the UK Science Research Council.

Similarly, the United States Naval Observatory (USNO) in Washington DC was established by the Secretary of the Navy as the Depot for Charts and Instruments; it later became responsible for

maintaining a time service. The USNO motto is based on a quotation from the Roman star atlas known as *The Astronomican*. The Latin quotation '*adde gubernandi stadium: pervenit in astra et pontum caelo coniunxit*' can be translated: 'then to the pilot's care: the stars are scaled, and sky with ocean joined'.

On the other hand, Dunsink Observatory, founded by Trinity College Dublin in 1783, was established to advance the academic pursuit of knowledge. However, Dunsink did contribute in several important ways to practical navigation. A chair of astronomy at Dublin was long overdue; Oxford had founded the Savilian Professorship of Astronomy in 1619 and Cambridge had two professorships: the Plumian chair (1704) and the Lowndean chair (1749).

In 1790, a second Irish observatory was founded in Armagh by Archbishop Richard Robinson

5.02—Greenwich Royal Observatory. CREATIVE COMMONS 2.0

5.03—Dunsink Observatory in 1835 by R. Havell & Son. NATIONAL LIBRARY IRELAND

(1708–94) of the Church of Ireland. Robinson was keen to establish a university of Ulster in Armagh and although he was responsible for the construction of many of the classical buildings in the city, he never achieved his ambition. However, the observatory prospered especially under the unrelated Revd Dr Thomas Romney Robinson (1792–1882) who was director for over 58 years. In 1846, Robinson invented a four-cup anemometer, which gave reliable measurements of wind speed and furthered the science of meteorology. The design was originally suggested to him by Richard Lovell

5.04—The domes of Armagh Observatory. NATIONAL LIBRARY IRELAND

5.05—Archbishop Richard Robinson. NATIONAL LIBRARY IRELAND

5.06—Four-cup
anemometer on the roof
of Armagh Observatory.
ARMAGH OBSERVATORY

5.07—Francis Andrews,
Provost of Trinity College
Dublin.

Edgeworth (1744–1817), his future father-in-law, and may have been motivated by the destructive Big Wind of January 1839.

The founding of an astronomical observatory in Dublin and the establishment of a chair of astronomy were aspirations of Francis Andrews (1718–74), a former Provost of Trinity College, who made a bequest for this purpose. Andrews, appointed Provost in 1758, was a lawyer and effective administrator. His tenure in office was harmonious and productive with the endowment of several new professorships. It saw the building of the Dining Hall and the Provost's House, which became the focus of his generous hospitality. Andrews died in 1774 but his will was contested by his relations and the legal battle dragged through the courts until August 1780.

In March 1781, William Herschel discovered a new object in the sky that he thought was a comet. Further observations over the next two years showed that it was a new planet, the first to be discovered apart from those known to the ancients. We know it as the gaseous giant planet Uranus. At a stroke Herschel's discovery doubled the size of the Solar System and gave a great stimulus to telescopic observations. It also may have encouraged the board of Trinity College to spare no expense in equipping the new observatory with the best available instruments. The Observatory cost £8000 in 1785, which was considerably more than Provost Andrews' endowment of a capital sum of £3000 and an annual sum of £250 'for ever'.

5.2 The 1st Andrews Professor of Astronomy, the Revd Dr Henry Ussher (1741–1790)

On 10 December 1783, Trinity College placed a contract with Mr Graham Moyers for the erection of the Dunsink Observatory. In January 1783, the Revd Henry Ussher was appointed the first Andrews Professor of Astronomy. Ussher had been a Senior Fellow of the College since 1781 and it appears that he had already chosen a site and drawn up plans for the Observatory. Ussher had a telescope at his home and he had a keen interest in meteorology. In 1784, he paid an extended visit to London to consult Nevil Maskelyne, the Astronomer Royal, and Jesse Ramsden, the famous instrument maker.

Nevil Maskelyne (1732–1811) is noted for his method of determining longitude using the position of the Moon, which became known as the lunar distance method. The Board of Longitude sent him to Barbados in 1763 to calculate the longitude of the capital, Bridgetown, by observations of Jupiter's moons and also to test his lunar distance method and compare its accuracy with John Harrison's chronometer, the No. 4 timekeeper. He was appointed the fifth Astronomer Royal in 1765 and as an experienced observer was in a good position to advise Henry Ussher about all aspects of the proposed observatory for Trinity College Dublin.

Jesse Ramsden (1735–1800) was the foremost telescope maker of his time. He was renowned for the design, craftsmanship and the accuracy of his large instruments and he employed a workforce of 50 men. He was elected a Fellow of the Royal Society in 1786 and was awarded its Copley Medal in 1795 for his 'various inventions and improvements in philosophical instruments'. His most famous instrument, a five-foot vertical circle, was finished in 1789 for Giuseppe Piazzi at Palermo in Sicily. When the Palermo circle was half-completed, Maskelyne, Ussher and Ramsden together planned a larger circle ten feet in diameter for Dunsink. However, Ramsden and Ussher quarrelled and Ramsden vowed that Ussher would never receive the completed instrument.

Ussher's plans for the observatory were well informed and innovative. He chose a site on top of the hill at Dunsink, north of the Phoenix Park, with clear views all around and open to the prevailing south-westerly winds. To avoid transmitting external vibrations to the telescopes, he made sure the telescope piers had firm foundations that were independent of the foundations of the outside walls. The original plan shows a central block and dome flanked by wings, each with a smaller dome, extending along a north–south axis. The central block formed the director's residence and behind it to the west was the Meridian where the transits of stars were observed and timed. The Meridian Room was equipped with shutters that were opened to view the sky and special openings in the walls allowed air to circulate around the telescopes. All these precautions were taken to ensure that the star images were as sharp and steady as possible. In June 1785, Ussher read a paper to the Royal Irish Academy about the choice of site and the design of the building; this was published as the first

5.08—Instrument-maker
Jesse Ramsden in 1790.

Painted by R. Home

Engraved by John Jones

contribution to the *Transactions* of the Academy.

The observatory was completed in 1785 and Ussher made his first observations in August that year. Dunsink never acquired its north and south wings, probably on account of the extra expense incurred by the legal proceedings. At its opening, it also lacked its main instrument, the great transit circle, originally intended to be ten feet in diameter, and a pair of precision clocks ordered from John Arnold (1736–99), the famous clock and watch maker. Ussher set up a four-foot transit circle with a six-foot telescope of 4.1-inch aperture, made by Ramsden for 200 guineas, and he had a clock by Crosthwaite of Dublin to time the astronomical transits.

The following summer he was joined by a 14-year-old lad who had a passion for the sea; this was Francis Beaufort, born in Navan, and son of the Revd Daniel Beaufort, a noted map maker and a former neighbour on Mecklenberg Street, Dublin (now

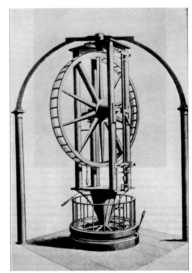

5.09—The Palermo 5-foot circle. MUNICH DIGITAL LIBRARY

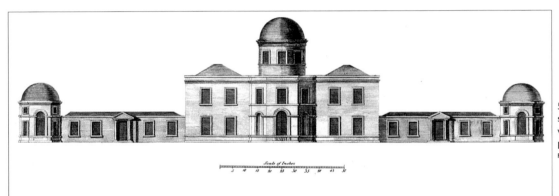

ELEVATION of East front of the OBSERVATORY belonging to Trinity College DUBLIN.

5.10—Drawing of Dunsink showing two side wings, as it was originally planned. DUBLIN INSTITUTE FOR ADVANCED STUDIES

Railway St., which runs from Gardiner St. to Portland Row). Francis was a keen pupil and during his five month's stay (1 July–7 December) he acquired the rudiments of astronomy and meteorology. These were of inestimable value to him in his career in the British Navy.

Two months before his fifteenth birthday, Francis set off on his first voyage aboard a British East India Company's ship bound for China. The ship ran aground near Jakarta and Francis experienced his first shipwreck. His next posting was as a midshipman in the Royal Navy and during

5.11—Dunsink as it was completed in 1785 with just the central block. NATIONAL LIBRARY IRELAND

5.12—Rear-Admiral Sir Francis Beaufort.

the Napoleonic Wars he rose to lieutenant and then commander by 1800. When serving on HMS *Phaeton* he was badly wounded; during his convalescence he helped his brother-in-law, Richard Lovell Edgeworth, construct a semaphore line from Dublin to Galway.

The Admiralty gave Beaufort as his first command HMS *Woolwich* and requested him to conduct a hydrographic survey of the Rio de la Plata estuary in South America. This he did in exemplary fashion and he gained a reputation for accuracy and perseverance. Beaufort went on to survey many uncharted seas and on his retirement in 1829 at the age of 55 was appointed hydrographer of the British Navy, a post he held for 26 years. Beaufort converted a minor chart repository into the finest surveying institution in the world and Admiralty charts became a byword for accuracy and reliability.

Beaufort trained Robert Fitzroy who was appointed commander for the second famous voyage of the survey ship HMS *Beagle*. Fitzroy asked for a scientific companion and Beaufort's enquiries led to Charles Darwin joining the expedition and eventually to the publication of *The Origin of Species*.

Beaufort is probably best known for his wind scale, which classifies the velocity and force of wind at sea. His name appears on maps of the world for places such as the Beaufort Sea in the Arctic Ocean, Beaufort Island in the Antarctic and Beaufort Inlet in the North Atlantic. He was elected a Fellow of the Royal Society in 1814 and he was appointed KCB in 1848. Although his name is most frequently associated with his wind scale, which he proposed in 1806, all who travel the seas have reason to be thankful to him for the high standards he set for the charts produced under his supervision. He died on 17 December 1857 aged 83 at Hove in Sussex and he is buried in St John's Church Gardens, London.

Ussher had a family of three sons and four daughters. His eldest son, Thomas (1779–1848), had a distinguished career in the British Royal Navy, serving with distinction in the French Revolutionary and Napoleonic Wars. In 1814, as Captain of HMS *Undaunted*, he conveyed Napoleon Bonaparte into exile in Elba. Napoleon gave him gifts of his own Friedlander telescope bearing his arms and a snuff box containing a miniature portrait of the emperor surrounded by diamonds. George IV once offered him £3,000 for the snuff box and a private individual a much larger sum.

5.3 The 2nd Andrews Professor, the Revd Dr John Brinkley (1766–1835)

Ussher died in May 1790 and was replaced by John Brinkley from Greenwich on the recommendation of Maskelyne and with the vigorous support of the Provost, John Hely-Hutchinson. As part of a campaign to put Dunsink on the map, Provost Hely-Hutchinson succeeded in having Brinkley and each subsequent Andrews professor recognised as the 'Royal Astronomer of Ireland' by letters patent of George III in 1792. However, the title 'Astronomer Royal' was frequently used, even by those who themselves held the position. Brinkley had to wait until 1808 for delivery of the Great Ramsden Circle; it had to be reduced in size to eight feet and was completed by Ramsden's pupil and successor, Matthew Berge.

With the Great Circle and the clocks in place, Brinkley started upon his life's work, the determination of stellar parallax. He chose to concentrate on observing four bright stars and he claimed to have measured a parallax of nearly one arc-second but this was disputed by John Pond, the Astronomer Royal, and led to a lengthy controversy. Eventually the verdict went against Brinkley but the methods he developed for reducing the data were of great benefit to later observers. The first convincing determination of the distance of a star by parallax was eventually made by F.W. Bessel of Königsberg (now Kaliningrad) in 1838.

Brinkley's mathematical ability enabled him to make important contributions to theoretical astronomy and he derived new values for important constants. He was also an inspiring teacher and his *Elements of Plane Astronomy* (1808) was the first astronomical textbook in the English language. Brinkley had been ordained priest in the Church of England in 1791 and finding his professorial salary inadequate, he followed a parallel ecclesiastical career in the Church of Ireland, becoming a recognized authority on ecclesiastical law. After holding several sinecures, he was appointed bishop of Cloyne, Co. Cork, in 1826.

5.13—The Great
Ramsden 8-foot circle.
SCIENCE PHOTO LIBRARY

5.14—The Revd Dr John Brinkley.
SCIENCE PHOTO LIBRARY

5.4 The 3rd Andrews Professor of Astronomy, Sir William Rowan Hamilton (1805–1865)

When the Trinity board moved to fill the vacant chair of astronomy, they took the unprecedented step of appointing a 21-year-old undergraduate who had not yet taken his final examinations. The new professor was William Rowan Hamilton who, apart from a brilliant academic record in classics and mathematics, had already established his reputation as a creative mathematician by submitting to the Royal Irish Academy a couple of months previously a paper on optics entitled Theory of Systems of Rays. Thus, on 16 June 1827, the youthful Hamilton became Andrews Professor of astronomy and Royal Astronomer of Ireland. He took up residence at Dunsink Observatory where he remained for the rest of his life, devoting all his energies to mathematics.

With a precision befitting a future mathematician, Hamilton had been born at midnight on 3/4 August 1805 in Dominick Street, Dublin. His father, Archibald, was a solicitor and close friend of the United Irishman, Archibald Hamilton Rowan after whom the boy was named. Before his third birthday William was sent to Trim to be educated by his uncle, the Revd James Hamilton, who was in charge of the diocesan school at Talbot Castle.

James was a Trinity graduate and a classical scholar with an interest in oriental languages. William was a precocious child and was soon reading the Bible in English. His uncle introduced him to Hebrew, Latin and Greek and his father hoped that his skill with languages would suit him for a career with the East India Company. When William was 10, Archibald boasted to a friend that his son knew Hebrew, Persian, Arabic, Sanscrit, Chaldee, Syriac, Hindoostanee, Malay, Mahratta and Bengali, in addition to Latin, Greek and the modern European languages.

By the age of 13 William had developed a talent for mental arithmetic but he could not beat the famous calculating prodigy Zerah Colburn from the United States. However, his failure seems to have triggered an interest in algebra and a shift from languages to mathematics. At 17 he discovered a mistake in Laplace's *Méchanique celeste,* which brought him to the attention of John Brinkley of Dunsink. This marked the start of his career as a creative mathematician.

Hamilton's mathematical work on the wave theory of light led him to predict in 1832 a new optical effect called conical refraction, which occurs when a beam of light strikes a biaxial crystal at a particular angle. A few months later the prediction was confirmed experimentally by Humphrey Lloyd, a Trinity colleague. This caused a sensation at the time for it demonstrated the predictive power of mathematics in science and it gained an international reputation for Hamilton. He later extended his mathematical methods to dynamics. He was twice awarded the prestigious Cunningham Medal of the Royal Irish Academy in 1834 and 1848, was knighted in 1835 and received the Royal Medal of the Royal Society in 1836.

In the 1920s, Hamilton's powerful mathematical tools were used by Erwin Schrödinger and others to develop the science of the sub-atomic world, which we know as quantum mechanics. Schrödinger described Hamilton's importance for his theory in the following terms:

The Hamiltonian principle has become the cornerstone of modern physics, the thing which a physicist expects every physical phenomenon to be in conformity. … The central conception of all modern theory in physics is 'The Hamiltonian'. If you wish to apply modern theory to any particular problem, you must start by putting the problem 'in Hamiltonian form'. Thus Hamilton is one of the greatest men of science the world has produced.

Hamilton considered his greatest achievement to have been his discovery of quaternions – an extension of the idea of complex numbers to four dimensions. A complex number ($a+ib$ where i is

5.15—Portrait of Sir
William Rowan Hamilton.

5.16—Hamilton's discovery of quaternions on 16 October 1843 at Broome Bridge.

√-1) may be considered as an ordered pair of real numbers (a,b) and they can be easily multiplied. Hamilton wanted to find a way to multiply triplets of real numbers (e.g., a,b,c) but a solution evaded him for many years. Eventually the answer came to him in a flash on 16 October 1843 as he was walking with his wife from Dunsink along the towpath of the Royal Canal towards Dublin to preside at a meeting of the Royal Irish Academy. He later wrote:

> I then and there felt the galvanic circuit of thought close; and the sparks which fell
> from it were the fundamental equations between i, j, k. ... I felt a problem to have been
> at that moment solved – an intellectual want relieved – which had haunted me for at
> least fifteen years before.

His discovery proved to be a turning point for algebraic theory because quaternions did not obey the commutative law of multiplication: $BA = AB$. With quaternions, the order was important and $BA = - AB$. The discovery of quaternions is commemorated by a plaque erected at Broome Bridge in 1958.

In recent years, quaternions have found many practical applications. They are widely used for three-dimensional modelling such as creating the character Lara Croft in the computer game Tomb Raider. Their ability to describe spatial rotations makes them useful in orbital mechanics and it is common for the attitude-control systems of spacecraft to be commanded in terms of quaternions.

Hamilton recorded the fundamental equations in his notebook and carved them with a knife on a stone of Broome Bridge, which was named after William Broome, a former director of the Royal Canal Company who lived nearby. Hamilton used to refer to the bridge as 'Brougham Bridge', which is pronounced the same way; this may have been because of his regard for Sir Henry Brougham, the Whig politician and designer of the four-wheeled, horse-drawn carriage that bears his name. Hamilton's mother Sarah was a Hutton and a member of the Dublin coach-making firm of Summerhill in Dublin that constructed the Irish State Coach for Queen Victoria in 1853.

Hamilton had a great love of poetry and often expressed himself in sonnets. He first met the poet Wordsworth in 1827 and they exchanged letters regularly. One of Hamilton's sisters, Eliza, wrote poetry also and when Wordsworth visited Dunsink, it was her poems that he liked rather than Hamilton's. The two men had long debates about science and poetry. Wordsworth had to tell Hamilton quite forcibly that his talents lay in science rather than poetry:

> You send me showers of verses which I receive with much pleasure ... yet have we fears that this employment may seduce you from the path of science. ... Again I do venture to submit to your consideration, whether the poetical parts of your nature would not find a field more favourable to their nature in the regions of prose, not because those regions are humbler, but because they may be gracefully and profitably trod, with footsteps less careful and in measures less elaborate.

Although Hamilton attempted to make regular astronomical observations in his early years at Dunsink, he soon delegated them to his observing assistant and to his sisters who lived with him in Observatory House until his marriage. The Revd Thomas Romney Robinson, director of Armagh Observatory, despaired of Hamilton as a practical observer. Hamilton's personal life was not happy; he was unlucky in love, he had an unfortunate marriage and he struggled with alcoholism in his later years.

Hamilton had a number of idiosyncrasies. His elder son William Edwin recounted:

> He used to carry on long trains of algebraic and arithmetical calculations in his mind, during which he was unconscious of the earthly necessity of eating; we used to bring in a 'snack' and leave it in his study, but a brief nod of recognition of the intrusion of the chop or cutlet was often the only result, and his thoughts went on soaring upwards.

Sir Robert Ball wrote of Hamilton:

> He was endowed with two distinct voices, one a high treble, the other a deep bass, and he alternately employed these voices not only in ordinary conversation, but when he was delivering an address on the profundities of Quaternions to the Royal Irish Academy, or on similar occasions. His friends had long grown so familiar with this peculiarity that they were sometimes rather surprised to find how ludicrous it appeared to strangers.

When Dr Piazzi Smyth of Edinburgh visited Dunsink in 1872, he was told that Hamilton when

5.17—William Hamilton
with one of his sons,
c.1845.

young was said to have hopped on one leg all around the top parapet of the Observatory.

A measure of Hamilton's international status is given by the fact that when the American National Academy of Sciences was established in 1885, he headed its list of Foreign Associates. Hamilton received the news of this honour a few months before his death on 2 September 1865.

5.5 The 4th Andrews Professor of Astronomy, Dr Franz F.E. Brünnow (1821–1891)

Hamilton was succeeded by Franz Brünnow (pronounced *brew-nuv*), the Berlin-born director of Ann Arbor Observatory in Michigan who revived observational work at Dunsink.

After graduating with a PhD in Berlin, Brünnow had worked under Enke at the Berlin Observatory. Brünnow was present when Galle discovered the planet Neptune on 23 September 1846. In 1851, he wrote the textbook *Lehrbuch der Sphärischen Astronomie*, which he translated into English himself in 1865 as *Handbook of Spherical Astronomy*. He was recruited by University of Michigan president Henry Tappan and came to Ann Arbor in 1854 where he accepted the post of director of the new observatory. He married Tappan's daughter Rebecca in 1867. When Tappen was

5.18—Sir James South.
SCIENCE PHOTO LIBRARY

dismissed by the University's regents, Brünnow resigned and returned to Germany.

In 1863, when William Parsons, third Earl of Rosse, was installed as Chancellor of Dublin University (Trinity College), Robinson of Armagh persuaded his friend Sir James South (1785–1867) of London to donate a fine 12-inch lens to the university. In 1868, the 12-inch lens was mounted in a telescope mounting made years earlier by Thomas Grubb and was installed in a fine granite building with a dome in the grounds of the Observatory. Brünnow commissioned the South

Equatorial and used it for research on stellar parallax. The James South Equatorial Telescope still has the distinction of being the largest refracting telescope in Ireland and it gave countless visitors to the observatory's open nights the thrill of viewing the night sky.

In 1873, Brünnow ordered and installed a first-class transit circle made by Pistor and Martins of Berlin similar to the one that he had used in Ann Arbour. It was capable of a four-fold increase of accuracy compared to the Ramsden Circle. The South telescope was also equipped with a double-wire micrometer for measuring the separation and position angle of visual double stars.

After nine years at Dunsink, Brünnow's failing health and eyesight caused him to resign. He retired to Basel and eventually to Heidelberg, where he died in 1891. In retirement he occupied himself with music for which he had a great talent.

5.6 The 5th Andrews Professor of Astronomy, Sir Robert S. Ball (1840–1913)

Brünnow was succeeded in 1874 by Robert S. Ball, who became well known for his public lectures and popular books. He was a talented mathematician and his work on the dynamics of rigid bodies earned him Fellowship of the Royal Society and the Cunningham Medal of the Royal Irish Academy.

Robert Ball was born on 1 July 1840 at 3 Granby Row, Dublin. His father, also Robert, was the

Honorary Secretary of the Royal Zoological Society and he worked hard for Dublin Zoo. After attending schools in Dublin and Chester, Robert jun. entered Trinity College Dublin where he was a very diligent student. He graduated in 1861 with two gold medals – one in Mathematics and the other in Experimental and Natural Sciences. After three attempts at Fellowship in Trinity, Ball was offered the post of tutor to the three youngest sons of the 3rd Earl of Rosse at Birr Castle on the understanding that he could observe with the great 72-inch reflector.

In 1867, Ball was appointed Professor of Applied Mechanics at the newly established Royal College of Science in Dublin where he developed his great aptitude for lecturing. It was about this time also that he became interested in the mathematical theory of small oscillations of a rigid body that developed into his 'Theory of Screws'. For this work he was elected to the Royal Society in 1873 and was later awarded the Cunningham Medal of the Royal Irish Academy.

In 1874, Ball was appointed Andrews Professor of Astronomy and Royal Astronomer of Ireland at Dunsink Observatory. He continued the difficult investigations on parallax that had been undertaken by his predecessors and he used the 12-inch South refractor to study the orbits of binary stars.

5.20—*Spy* cartoon of Robert Ball.

5.21—The first Fastnet lighthouse under construction.

He became an accomplished public speaker and frequently travelled to England to address packed halls. It is estimated that in Britain alone a total of over a million people attended his public lectures and many more read some of his 13 popular books on astronomy. He was Victorian England's version of the popular astronomer Patrick Moore and became a celebrity with his cartoon by Spy (Leslie Ward) appearing in *Vanity Fair* in 1904. He undertook three lecture tours of the United States and Canada, which were resounding successes. On several occasions he gave the Christmas Lectures at the Royal Institution in London. In 1886, he was knighted by the Lord Lieutenant of Ireland.

Ball served as Scientific Adviser to the Irish Lights Board from 1882 to 1912 and advised the board on all technical matters that arose. For instance, in 1884 he compared the relative merits of gas, electricity and oil as lighthouse light sources. He took great delight in joining the annual inspections, which involved circumnavigating the coast of Ireland. During the inspections, he took more than 1000 photographs including 500 panoramic ones and these are in the custody of the National Photographic Archive. The Archive mounted an exhibition of Ball's photographs in 2003 entitled *For the Safety of All* and published a book of the same name. His photographs include a record of the building (from 1897 to 1904) of the second Fastnet lighthouse, which he described as the most beautiful in the world.

In 1892, Ball was appointed Lowndean Professor of Astronomy and Geometry and director of the Observatory at Cambridge. Unfortunately, his eyesight gradually deteriorated and he lost his right eye in 1897; this did not prevent him playing golf! Despite this handicap, he continued to divide his time between his official duties, his mathematical research and his activities as a public lecturer and author of many popular books on astronomy. He died at the age of 73 after a long illness and was buried in St. Giles churchyard in Cambridge.

5.7 The 6th Andrews Professor of Astronomy, Dr Arthur A. Rambaut (1859–1923)

When Sir Robert Ball moved to Cambridge in 1892, he was succeeded by his assistant, Dr Arthur Rambaut, who was an accomplished observer as well as an excellent mathematician.

Both Ball and Rambaut were involved in planning the refurbishment of a 15-inch reflector that had been donated by Isaac Roberts in 1888. The reflector was remounted, modernised and equipped with a new dome by Howard Grubb of Rathmines and from 1895 was used for stellar photography. In 1897, Rambaut moved to the Radcliffe Observatory in Oxford where he had a distinguished career.

5.8 The 7th Andrews Professor of Astronomy, Dr Charles J. Joly (1864–1906)

Rambaut was succeeded by Dr Charles Jasper Joly, second cousin of the geologist and physicist, John Joly. As a Fellow of Trinity, C.J. Joly had an established reputation as a productive mathematician and had applied Hamilton's quaternion methods to complex geometrical problems. At Dunsink, Joly continued this line of research and in 1905 he published a *Manual of Quaternions,* which superseded all other introductory works on the subject. Joly also directed much observational work the results of which appeared in the publication *Dunsink Observations and Researches.*

In May 1900, Rambaut and Joly took part in the joint Royal Irish Academy – Royal Dublin Society total eclipse expedition to Plasencia in Spain, which obtained some excellent photographs of the eclipsed Sun. The adjacent photograph shows Joly adjusting a long-focus solar camera. The camera was fed a beam of sunlight from a heliostat made by Howard Grubb of the famous telescope-

5.22—Charles Joly focusing a solar camera to photograph the total eclipse of the sun at Plasencia, Spain, May 1900.

making firm in Rathmines. A heliostat has a flat mirror that is rotated to compensate for the Earth's rotation. Grubb made two of these 8-inch heliostats for the RIA-RDS expedition and one of them was subsequently used in the 1919 total eclipse expedition to Sobral in Brazil. The 8-inch heliostat and a 4-inch lens on loan from the Royal Irish Academy provided crucial data that showed that a beam of starlight was deflected by the Sun's gravitational field by an amount consistent with Albert Einstein's General Theory of Relativity. Overnight, Einstein became a celebrity and the world's most famous scientist.

5.9 The 8th Andrews Professor of Astronomy, Sir Edmund T. Whittaker (1873–1956)

The next resident of Dunsink was Edmund T. Whittaker who had excelled in mathematics at Cambridge University. Whittaker made a considerable impact on the scientific life of Dublin through his lectures and social contacts. Using the 15-inch Roberts reflector, he began a programme of systematic photographic observations of variable stars. During his time at Dunsink, he also published his influential book on the *History of the Theories of the Aether and Electricity*, which he revised in 1952–53. In 1912, he was appointed professor of mathematics in Edinburgh, where he taught until his retirement in 1946 and where he established a flourishing research school.

5.10 The 9th Andrews Professor of Astronomy, Dr Henry C. Plummer (1875–1946)

Whittaker was followed by Henry C.K. Plummer, an astronomer and mathematician from Oxford. Plummer continued the observations of variable stars and suggested in 1913 that the variability of some stars might be due to pulsations; this idea was later developed in a fruitful way by Sir Arthur

Eddington. In 1921, Plummer was appointed professor of mathematics at the Artillery College, Woolwich, in London. The Trinity board decided to leave the vacant post unfilled as the college's finances were under considerable strain in the years of the Civil War (1921–23) and its aftermath. The Assistant Director, Charles Martin, became Acting Director and maintained the time service with the assistance of F.J. O'Connor who also lectured in Trinity College. Martin died in June 1936 and the observatory closed in mid-1937. During the 'Emergency' of WW II, 1939–45, the observatory buildings were rented to Dr R.M. Gwynn SFTCD and to Dr Oliver Chance, a medical consultant.

5.11 Decline and Renewal at Dunsink Observatory

Charles Martin had come to Dunsink at the age of 22 in 1895 from the Royal Observatory, Greenwich. He served under Rambaut, Joly, Whittaker and Plummer and during those years he was primarily responsible for observing the clock stars and keeping the time signals operating. With Whittaker and Plummer, he also made photographic observations to measure the brightness of stars. From 1921, caretakers occupied the main observatory building and Mr Martin, his wife and two daughters continued to occupy the Assistant's House. He was interested in long-distance aviation and he planned the course taken by the first successful east–west Atlantic flight by Baron von Hünefeld, Capt. Kohl and Major Fitzmaurice in April 1928. He died in June 1936 having served the Observatory for 41 years.

5.23—Charles Martin who served at Dunsink for 41 years. DUNSINK OBSERVATORY

The time service was then maintained by F.J. O'Connor, a TCD lecturer, who had assisted Martin since 1924. In November 1936, the TCD Registrar informed the Port and Docks Board that the time service would be terminated with effect from 1 August 1937; this signalled the temporary closure of Dunsink Observatory.

For a decade the observatory lay dormant but not forgotten. Dunsink's closure seriously concerned the Taoiseach, Éamon de Valera (1882–1975) who, as a young man, had lectured in mathematics at Carysfort training college for teachers and at St Patrick's College, Maynooth. He had attended Whittaker's lectures in Trinity College between 1906 and 1908 and had come to appreciate the great contributions that Hamilton had made to mathematics. The two men established a strong bond of friendship. On 13 November 1908,

Whittaker wrote the following testimonial:

> Mr Edward [sic] de Valera has attended several of my Professorial Courses of lectures
> on Spectroscopy, Astrophysics, and Electro-Optics during the past two years. In the
> personal intercourse which has thus been brought about, I have been much impressed
> by the intellectual vigour with which he has interested himself in the most difficult
> problems of Natural Philosophy. His knowledge is both broad and deep, and I am
> confident that in any educational position he will exercise the best of influences over
> those with whom he is brought in contact.
>
> Edmund T. Whittaker, Sc.D, F.R.S. Royal Astronomer of Ireland

5.12 The Dublin Institute for Advanced Studies

De Valera became head of the government of the Irish Free State in 1932. After the adoption of the
Irish Constitution in 1937, he became Taoiseach. He wished to make a lasting contribution to Irish
culture by setting up an institution modelled on the lines of the Institute for Advanced Study at
Princeton. After consultations with various academics, including Whittaker, the Dublin Institute for
Advanced Studies Act came into force in June 1940. Initially the Institute had two Schools: Celtic
Studies and Theoretical Physics. The first senior professor of Theoretical Physics was the Nobel
Laureate Erwin Schrödinger who had fled Austria in April 1938. Schrödinger's standing has since
been somewhat overshadowed by revelations about his private life.

In 1942, Dr Eric Lindsay, director of Armagh Observatory, suggested reopening Dunsink as a
working observatory, with access to a telescope at Bloemfontein, South Africa, owned jointly by
Armagh, Dunsink and Harvard observatories. In March 1947, the third School, of Cosmic Physics,
was added to the Institute. Initially it had three sections, which were Astrophysical, Cosmic Ray and
Meteorological, each in charge of a senior professor. Subsequently, the sections were renamed the
Astronomy, Cosmic Ray and Geophysics Sections. The Government bought Dunsink from Trinity
and the School of Cosmic Physics was located there in March 1947. The Schools of Celtic Studies
and Theoretical Physics were accommodated at No 5 Merrion Square.

The first Senior Professor of the Astrophysical Section was Hermann A. Brück (1905–2000),
originally from Prussia, and also a refugee from the Nazis. Brück took up residence at Dunsink in
October 1947 and immediately started reconstructing and re-equipping the observatory. Brück
became a well-known figure around Dublin and started the regeneration of interest in astronomy.
He was largely responsible for organising the prestigious ninth general assembly of the International
Astronomical Union in Dublin in 1955. In October 1957, he moved to Edinburgh to become the
Astronomer Royal for Scotland and to direct the Royal Observatory.

Brück was succeeded by Mervyn A. Ellison (1920–63), an expert on solar physics from the Royal
Observatory, Edinburgh, and the son of a former director of Armagh Observatory. While still at
Edinburgh, Ellison had set up an automatic solar telescope at the Royal Observatory, Cape of Good
Hope, to take advantage of the clear South African skies. The telescope took pictures of the full disk
of the Sun at one-minute intervals to monitor activity, especially the eruptions known as solar flares.
Ellison was also World Reporter for Solar Activity of the International Geophysical Year (July 1957
to December 1958). At the conclusion of the International Geophysical Year, Ellison had the onerous
task of organising the publication of the daily records of solar activity over the 18 months of the
project. In 1963, Ellison was making plans to participate in the forthcoming International Year of
the Quiet Sun but he became ill and died in September at the age of only 54.

5.24—Taoiseach Éamon de Valera (centre) who was instrumental in setting up the Dublin Institute for Advanced Studies. Dublin Port Archive

The next Senior Professor, Patrick A. Wayman (1927–98), from the Royal Greenwich Observatory at Herstmonceux in Sussex, took up residence at Dunsink in August 1964. Wayman continued the policy of using overseas observing facilities, first at Bloemfontein in South Africa and later at La Palma in the Canary Islands. In 1984, Trinity revived the Andrews Professorship of Astronomy and appointed Wayman to the Chair in an honorary capacity. He took a particular interest in the historical development of astronomy in Ireland and published his definitive history of Dunsink Observatory in 1987. As General Secretary of the International Astronomical Union from 1979 to 1982, he made important contributions; these included setting up a permanent secretariat in Paris and solving the long-standing problem of the adherence of the two parts of China to the Union.

After Wayman's retirement in 1992, Evert J.A. Meurs was appointed senior professor. His interests lay mainly in the violent events that take place near the centres of distant galaxies, which are believed to be connected with massive black holes. Observations cover the entire electromagnetic spectrum, ranging from gamma rays to radio waves and are obtained not only from ground-based observatories but from many space-borne observatories. In addition, huge databases are accessible through the internet and searching these is known as 'data mining'. He retired in 2000.

The fact that astronomical research no longer depends on the particular location of Dunsink led the Institute to merge the Astronomical Section at Dunsink with the Astrophysical Section (formerly the Cosmic Ray Section) at 31 Fitzwilliam Place in Dublin. The Institute plans to retain Dunsink Observatory as a conference centre and for educational outreach. The intention is to create a centre to promote both mathematics and the physical sciences that underpin our knowledge-based economy. Dunsink Observatory's new purpose is to interpret the great discoveries of science and technology.

6. Atomic Time and the Global Positioning System

And he shall judge among the nations, and shall rebuke many people: and they shall beat their swords into plowshares, and their spears into pruning hooks: nation shall not lift up sword against nation, neither shall they learn war any more.

Isaiah 2:4

6.1

It is a sobering thought that the technology that moves shipping containers so efficiently around the world's oceans depends on the ability to make clocks with nanosecond accuracy, to build satellites and deploy them in earth orbit and to design and programme electronic computers.

6.01—The container ship *Sophia* at Dublin Port. DENIS BERGIN, DUBLIN PORT ARCHIVE, 2014

6.2 War and Peace

It is one of the ironies of history that technologies developed for death and destruction in the heat of war can bring great benefits to peacetime civilian life. For instance, the jet engine was invented independently in Britain and Germany in the 1930s and it influenced the latter years of World War II.

In 1928, a RAF cadet, Frank Whittle, submitted his ideas for a turbo-jet engine to his superiors. After developing his design, he was granted a patent in 1932. By April 1937, he had his first engine running and it flew in a test plane on 15 May 1941. It eventually became the Gloster Meteor jet fighter. In Germany in 1935, Hans von Ohain started work on a jet engine similar to Whittle's but unaware of his work. His design was adopted by Heinkel and the HE178 fighter was the first turbo-jet aircraft to fly in August 1939.

6.02—Gloster Meteor aircraft.

6.03—A replica of the Heinkel HE178V-1 jet aircraft in the Planes of Fame Museum, California, US. ALAN WILSON, CREATIVE COMMONS 2.0

The fact that jet engines were efficient at high speeds and high altitudes meant they were well suited to passenger aircraft so from the 1960s onwards all large civil aircraft were jet powered. By 2012, there were over 22,000 commercial jet aircraft in service and this number rose considerably in subsequent years. Some estimates forecast that the world's commercial aircraft numbers will rise to over 49,000 by 2039.

6.04—Frank Whittle and Hans von Ohain who each designed jet engines.

6.05—Sir Robert A. Watson-Watt.

6.3 Radar

Radar was developed in secret by several countries before and during World War II. The term is an acronym for RAdio Detection And Ranging. A radar dish or antenna emits microwave pulses that bounce off any object in their path and the time lag of the echo is a measure of the distance of the object. Britain was the first country to fully exploit radar for defence against attacking enemy aircraft. A team led by Robert Watson Watt (1892–1973) established a chain of radar towers along the east and south coasts of England; these were crucial in the winning of the Battle of Britain in 1940.

A key component of a radar set is its microwave generator for generating electromagnetic waves. Between 1937 and 1940, a British team built a multi-cavity magnetron but the microwaves that it generated at 150cm were too long and weak for adequate

6.06—The original Randall and Boot cavity magnetron. GENI, CREATIVE COMMONS

detection. The problem was solved in 1940 by John Randall and Harry Boot at the University of Birmingham who developed a high-power magnetron working at centimetre wavelengths. The cavity magnetron was credited with giving Allied radars a considerable performance advantage over enemy radars. It was later described by an American historian as 'the most valuable cargo ever brought to our shores'.

In peacetime, radar has proved to be vital for navigation, especially in fog or at night. Nowadays, all ships and even many small boats are fitted with radar. Airports are equipped with radar to assist air traffic controllers guide airplanes to safe take-off and landing in all weather conditions. The idea of using microwave energy to cook food was discovered accidently by Percy LeBaron Spencer of Raytheon who found that radar waves had melted a chocolate bar in his pocket.

6.4 Electronic Computers

The original meaning of the word 'computer' was a person who did calculations. Mechanical devices to aid human computers were called 'calculating machines' and these were widely used. During World War II the need arose for machines to perform very lengthy and complex calculations and electronic circuits provided the means to speed up the calculations.

The first programmable computing device was called Colossus and was built in 1943 by Tommy Flowers and his team at the Post Office Research Station in London. Its purpose was to assist the code breakers at Bletchley Park, a secret establishment that intercepted enemy messages. Colossus Mark I was delivered to Bletchley Park in January 1944 and it played an important role in the preparations for the Normandy landings. It had some 1600 thermionic valves to perform Boolean operations and calculations; an improved version, Colossus Mark II, had 2400 valves and was five times faster.

6.07—Bletchley Park, WWII code-breaking centre.

6.08—A Colossus Mark 2 code-breaking computer being operated by Dorothy Du Boisson (left) and Elsie Booker (right), 1943.

Ten Colossus computers were constructed. Details of their existence, design and use were kept secret until the late 1970s so Flowers and his team never received credit for their invention. At the end of the war, Winston Churchill ordered their destruction into pieces no larger than a man's hand, in order not to reveal Britain's ability to crack codes. Two of the Colossus computers were transferred to the newly formed GCHQ; they were dismantled in 1959–60. A functioning replica of a Colossus computer was completed in 2007 and is on display at the National Museum of Computing at Bletchley Park.

In the United States several electromechanical and electronic computers were constructed between 1937 and 1939 but none were programmable. The ENIAC (Electronic Numerical Integrator and Computer) was the first general-purpose electronic computer that could be programmed for many different tasks. It was built at the University of Pennsylvania between 1943 and 1945. It weighed 30 tons, used 160kW of electrical power and contained over 18,000 thermionic valves. One major problem was the replacement of burned-out valves.

ENIAC was sponsored by the US Army, which needed it to calculate artillery-firing tables. In one second, it could perform 5000 additions, 357 multiplications or 38 divisions. It cost US$500,000 and by the time it was completed the war was over. However, it was used for designing a hydrogen bomb, weather prediction, cosmic-ray studies and wind tunnel design. It was shut down on 2 October 1955.

6.5 Rockets

From June to October 1944, south-east England was subjected to terror bombing by the V-1 flying bomb, a jet-powered version of the cruise missile. Then, from September 1944, Germany launched over 3000 V-2 ballistic missiles against the Allies, targeted mainly at London and Antwerp. The attacks resulted in about 9000 deaths, both civilian and military.

When Germany was defeated, both the United States and the Soviet Union took advantage of the German expertise in rocketry so German men and equipment laid the foundation for the space race between the superpowers. The V-2 rocket was the brainchild of Werner von Braun, a brilliant

6.09—Picture of a V-1 flying bomb at the Royal Danish Arsenal Museum. KIM BACH, CREATIVE COMMONS 4.0

German engineer who had completed his doctoral thesis in 1934 on the design of liquid propelled rockets. Von Braun and 120 of his engineers moved to the United States and formed the nucleus of the American space effort.

6.6 Artificial Satellites

As part of the International Geophysical Year (1 July 1957–31 December 1958), both the United States and the Soviet Union planned to launch an artificial satellite into orbit around the Earth. Soviet superiority in rocket technology was demonstrated by the launch on 4 October 1957 of Sputnik 1, the first artificial satellite of the Earth. It was an aluminium sphere about 58cm in diameter fitted with four radio aerials and weighing nearly 84kg. It orbited the Earth every 96 minutes and stayed in orbit for three months. Its radio transmitters sent out the famous 'bleep-bleep' signals for 21 days, heralding the beginning of the Space Age. Sputnik caught the world's attention and the American public off guard. The United States responded by establishing the National Aeronautics and Space Administration (NASA).

The Americans attempted to launch their first satellite, Vanguard, on 5 December 1957 but much to their chagrin the rocket exploded on the launch pad. On 31 January 1958, von Braun's US Army team successfully launched the Explorer 1 satellite. It led to the discovery of the innermost of the

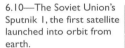

6.10—The Soviet Union's Sputnik 1, the first satellite launched into orbit from earth.

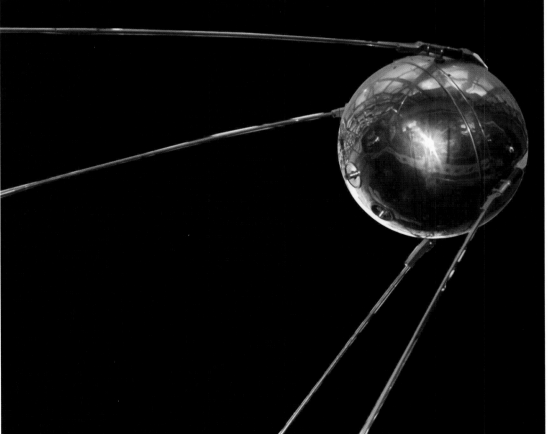

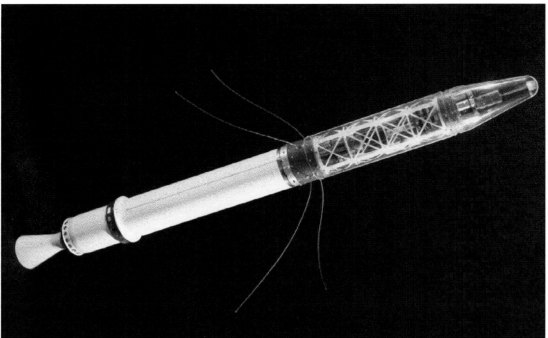

6.11—Explorer 1, the US space satellite launched in 1958.

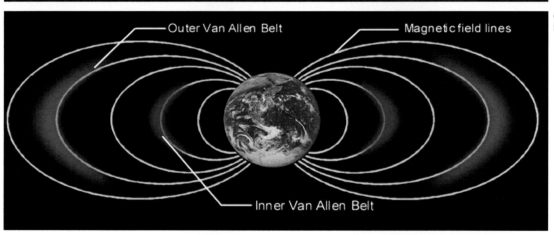

6.12—The Van Allen Radiation Belts.

Van Allen radiation belts, two zones of charged particles that surround the Earth; this was the first major scientific discovery to be made with an artificial satellite.

Nowadays there are over 1000 operational spacecraft in orbit around the Earth. Half of these are in Low-Earth Orbit (LEO), just a few hundred kilometres above the surface of the Earth. About five per cent are in Medium-Earth Orbit (MEO), about 20,000km altitude, and the rest are in Geosynchronous Orbit (GEO) at about 36,000km. A satellite in geosynchronous orbit has an orbital period that matches the Earth's rotation relative to the stars and so it appears to hover over one place on the Earth. If the orbit lies directly over the equator, it is said to be geostationary.

6.13—The Hubble Space Telescope.

6.7 Low-Earth Orbit Satellites

The LEO satellites include the International Space Station (ISS) at 370km, which was launched on 20 November 1998 at a cost of US$150 billion. A little higher up, at 559km, is the Hubble Space Telescope (HST), launched on 24 April 1990 at a cost of US$2.5 billion.Even higher, at 780km altitude, an armada of nearly 70 Iridium satellites provide global voice and data transfer.The relatively low altitude of the ISS and the HST ensures that they are accessible for exchange of crews and servicing. However, the resistance of the Earth's atmosphere causes the orbits to spiral towards the Earth unless corrected.

6.8 Medium-Earth Orbit Satellites

About one-twentieth of spacecraft are in Medium-Earth Orbit around 20,000km altitude and they are mainly for global navigation.Their motion through space is not affected by atmospheric drag. The United States operates the Global Positioning System (GPS), which consists of 24 satellites in six groups of four.The first GPS satellite was launched by the US Air Force in 1978 and the system has been continuously improved. GPS satellites will be discussed in more detail later in the chapter.

6.14—A GPS Navstar-2F satellite, part of the Global Positioning System (GPS).

6.9 Geosynchronous Satellites

At the end of 1928, the Austro-Hungarian rocket engineer Herman Potočnik set out a plan for establishing a space station with a human presence. He was the first to calculate a geostationary orbit in which the space station would keep pace with the Earth's rotation. Author Sir Arthur C. Clarke (1917–2008) is credited with proposing the notion of using a geostationary orbit for communications satellites.

Since geosynchronous satellites have the special property of remaining in the same position in the sky, it is easy for ground-based antennae to track them. There are about 600 geosynchronous satellites but not all of them are operational. One dis advantage of a high geosynchronous orbit

6.15—The writer Sir Arthur C. Clarke. MAMYJOMARASH

is the time lag for signals to travel to orbit and back. Radio signals take about a quarter of a second for the return journey; two people having a conversation will experience lags of half a second between comments. As a result, these satellites are used mainly for communications, television broadcasting and weather forecasting.

6.10 Atomic Clocks

An atomic clock uses a frequency standard that depends on electronic transitions between energy levels in an atom. Belfast-born Lord Kelvin and P.G. Tait were the first to point out in 1879 the advantage of using such natural standards. The first atomic clock, based on microwave resonances in ammonia, was built in 1949 at the US National Bureau of Standards (NBS); it was less accurate than the existing quartz clocks but served to demonstrate the principle. The first accurate atomic clocks using a transition of the isotope caesium-133 were built at the NBS and by Louis Essen (1908–97) at the National Physical Laboratory (NPL) in the UK. These advances led to the redefinition of the second in 1967 as the time it takes for an atom of caesium-133 to oscillate 9,192,631,770 cycles.

The second is now defined as the duration of 9,192,631,770 periods of the radiation corresponding to the transition between the two hyperfine levels of the ground state of the caesium-133 atom. The hyperfine structure arises from the interaction of the spin of the outer electron of the caesium atom and the spin of the nucleus. If the electron spin is in the same direction as the nuclear spin, the electron will have a slightly higher energy than if the spins lie in opposite directions. The transition between the two states gives rise to the 9.192 GHz radiation.

6.16—Louis Essen and his assistant with the NPL Caesium Clock. SCIENCE PHOTO LIBRARY

6.17—National Institute of Standards and Technology (NIST) experimental ytterbium clock. NATIONAL INSTITUTE OF STANDARDS AND TECHNOLOGY

6.18—Hoptroff pocket atomic watch. IMAGE COURTESY OF RICHARD HOPTROFF

The accuracy of atomic clocks has increased by a factor of a million in the past 60 years. Early atomic clocks were based on beams of atoms in microwave cavities at room temperature. Nowadays, a new form of atomic clock, the caesium fountain, is being used. Laser beams slow down and cool a cloud of atoms that is projected upwards in a microwave cavity and allowed to fall under gravity. The resonance transitions are measured while the atoms are in free fall. Other types of atoms have advantages. Rubidium clocks are smaller and cheaper and offer short-term stability; they are used commercially and for portable and aerospace applications. Hydrogen clocks have good short stability but lower long-term accuracy.

In August 2013, scientists at the US National Institute of Standards and Technology (NIST) announced that they had developed an ytterbium atomic clock that was stable to one part in 10^{18}; this is equivalent to one second in the age of the Universe. In contrast, NIST have also produced a miniature caesium atomic clock that is accurate to one part in 10^{10} and costs only \$1500; it will be a suitable time standard for places where GPS is unavailable such as in mines and under the sea. A commercial firm intends to produce a limited-edition pocket watch based on the same chip for the millionaire who has everything.

6.11 Radio Clocks

Apart from GPS, radio clocks enable everyone to access atomic time. For instance, the UK National Physical Laboratory (NPL) has three atomic clocks installed at Anthorn in Cumbria, which are synchronised with the UK time standard at NPL headquarters in Teddington. A long wave radio transmitter operating at 60kHz continuously broadcasts a time code that can be picked up within a radius of 1500km. The Anthorn transmitter replaced the old Rugby transmitter but retained its MSF call sign.

In the United States, the National Institute of Standards and Technology (NIST) has been operating a similar system since 1962 with the call sign WWVB at Fort Collins in Colorado. The NIST also operates a voice output short wave service with call sign WWV; it operates at 5, 10 and 15 MHz at high power and at 2.5 and 20MHz at low power. In 2011, NIST estimated the number of radio clocks and wristwatches equipped with WWVB receivers exceeded 50 million.

6.12 The Variable Rotation of the Earth

Since quartz clocks became available, it has been known that the rate of rotation of the Earth is irregular and it is, therefore, a poor timekeeper. Tidal friction accounts for a lengthening of the day by about two milliseconds per century. Post-glacial rebound of the continents shortens the day by 0.6 milliseconds per century. Seasonal winds cause a typical day in January to be about one millisecond longer than a typical day in June.

6.13 Co-ordinated Universal Time and Leap Seconds

In 1971, the name International Atomic Time (TAI) was assigned to a time scale based on SI seconds; the SI second is the base time unit in the International System of Units founded on the division of the day into hours, minutes and seconds. Irregularities in the time kept by atomic clocks were traced to the fact they were at different altitudes and consequently in different gravitational fields. According to the General Theory of Relativity, clocks in stronger gravitational fields (lower altitude) run slower. Starting from 1 January 1977, corrections were applied to atomic clocks so that TAI would correspond to time at mean sea level.

In order to take advantage of the accuracy of atomic clocks and to provide consistent civil time, GMT was replaced by Coordinated Universal Time (UTC) in 1963. The system was adjusted a number of times until 1972 when leap seconds were introduced to simplify future adjustments. The current version of UTC is based on TAI with leap seconds added at irregular intervals to compensate for Earth's variable rotation. Leap seconds keep UTC within 0.9 seconds of mean solar time at Greenwich. In the 42 years up to and including 2013, a total of 25 leap seconds were added.

The abbreviations TAI and UTC can be puzzling. International Atomic Time was originally proposed by the *Bureau International de l'Heure* in Paris, which regulates timekeeping worldwide. It proposed the French name *Temp Atomique International*, hence the acronym TAI. The official abbreviation for Coordinated Universal Time is UTC. This abbreviation arose from a desire by the International Telecommunication Union and the International Astronomical Union to use the same abbreviation in all languages. English speakers originally proposed CUT (for Coordinated Universal Time) while French speakers proposed TUC (for *Temps Universel Coordonné*). The compromise that emerged was UTC, which conforms to the pattern for the abbreviations of the variants of Universal Time (UT0, UT1, UT2, etc.)

6.14 The Global Positioning System

The Global Positioning System (GPS) was developed in the 1970s by the U.S. Department of Defence to provide a global navigation system for the U.S. Military forces. It consists of at least 24 satellites orbiting the Earth at an altitude of 20,000km. There are four satellites in each of six circular orbits. Each orbital plane is inclined at 55° to the equatorial plane and each satellite completes an orbit in about 12 hours, which means that it passes over any particular point on the Earth about twice a day. The first GPS satellite was launched in 1978 and full operational capability was achieved in April 1995.

The GPS satellites are powered by sun-seeking solar panels with nickel-cadmium batteries for storing energy. Each satellite has four caesium or rubidium clocks, only one of which is in use at a time. The clocks maintain UTC and time is counted in weeks and seconds from midnight on 5/6 January 1980. The clocks are accurate to about a nanosecond and are crucial for the proper operation of the system. The positions of the GPS satellites are continuously monitored by a worldwide network of ground stations, which report to a Master Control Station in Colorado Springs. The network maintains all the GPS clocks in synchronism.

To determine a position on Earth, a GPS receiver needs signals from at least four GPS satellites. The four signals are used to synchronize the receiver's quartz clock with the satellites' atomic clocks. Since both the satellites and the receiver are generating the same special sequence of pulses (known as pseudo random), the receiver can calculate the time lag for each of the satellite signals and hence the distance to each satellite. Simple geometry then gives the position of the receiver.

The precision achieved is exceptional: even a hand-held GPS receiver can determine its absolute position on the surface of the Earth to within five or ten metres in only a few seconds. With differential techniques, precision on the order of centimetres or millimetres in relative position can be obtained in under an hour or so.

6.15 GPS and Shipping Containers

The Global Positioning System has a multitude of applications but one of particular relevance to ports involves the loading and unloading of shipping containers. The technique is known as Differential GPS (DGPS) and it has revolutionized the transport of goods around the world.

6.19—GPS orbits around
Earth. MARTA LOPEZ ALARCÓN

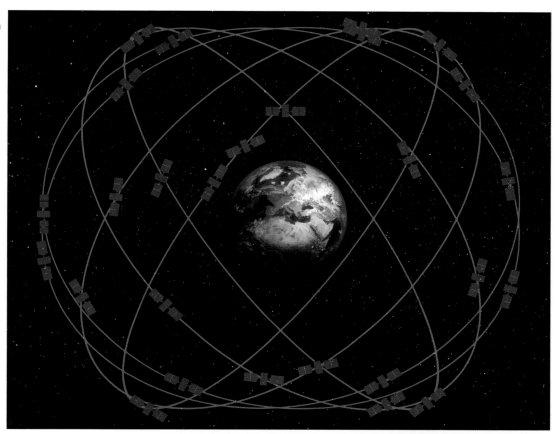

6.20—Civilian Magellan
Blazer12 GPS Receiver in
a marine application.
NACHOMAN-AU, CREATIVE
COMMONS 3.0

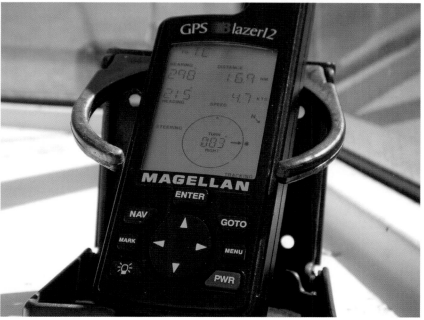

6.21—Container yard in the port of Bremerhaven, Germany. WOLFGANG KUNDEL, CREATIVE COMMONS 4.0

Shipping containers were first introduced in the 1950s but failed to make much impact because of a lack of standards. In the late 1960s, the International Organization for Standardization made recommendations on the dimensions, identity markings and corner fittings of general-purpose containers. Standard shipping containers are eight feet high by eight feet wide and may have lengths of 20, 40, 45, 48, or 53 feet. Each container has a unique identifier consisting of a 3-letter owner code, a 1-letter category code, a 6-digit serial number and a 1-digit check number. Containerization has eliminated the need for warehouses, reduced congestion in ports, shortened shipping time and reduced losses from damage and theft. There are approximately 17 million containers in the world of various types to suit different cargoes.

Like other ports in the world, Dublin port has had to phase out conventional cranes and stevedores and replace them with gantry cranes and large marshalling yards for the containers. Ports that lacked space to develop marshalling yards have gone into decline but Dublin was fortunate to have had sufficient space to accommodate the containers. The gantry cranes that are used in Dublin port are known as Rubber Tyred Gantries (RTGs) and each straddles many containers. The gantry has an overhead trolley that lifts a container with a framework known as a spreader and places the container in the required position.

The precise positioning of the containers is achieved with Differential GPS. A base station with a GPS receiver is located at a central position. Each RTG carries two GPS receivers and a radio aerial to communicate with the base station. By continuously monitoring the differential signals between the moving gantry and the fixed base station, the position of the gantry is known with an

6.22—The operation of Distributed GPS by a container gantry.

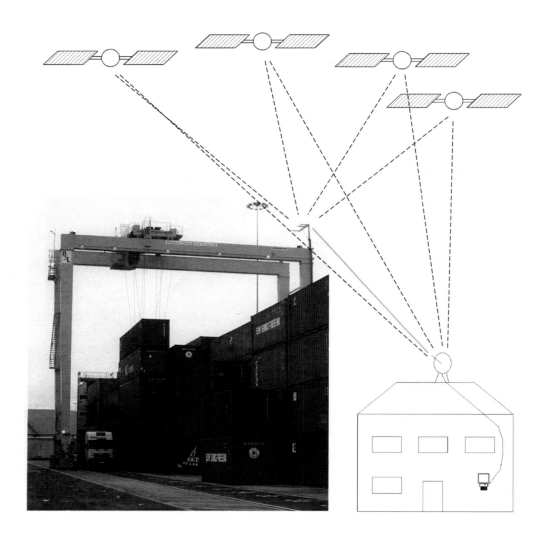

accuracy of about 30mm. The three-dimensional position of a container is given by the distance of the gantry along its track, the trolley position and the height of the spreader above ground level. After the spreader locks on to the corners of a container with twistlocks, it can be lifted and moved to where required. On releasing the twistlocks, the position of the container is recorded together with its size and weight.

6.16 GPS and Relativity

GPS is a good example of the practical importance of Einstein's theory of relativity. His Special Theory predicts that a clock moving relative to an observer runs slow; the GPS clocks lose about 7000ns or nanoseconds (7 s) each day because of their orbital velocity. His General Theory predicts that the GPS clocks should go about 45,000ns (40 s) faster because the Earth's gravitation field is weaker at high altitudes. To avoid having to make continual corrections for a net difference of 38,000ns a day, the GPS clocks are preset before launch to compensate for these relativistic effects.

6.17 Other Space Navigational Systems

Since the Global Positioning System has proved so important for military purposes, other nations are launching their own navigational systems. The European Union has been assembling since 2005 a satellite system called Galileo at an altitude of 23,000km. It will be under civilian control and will deliver positional accuracy of a metre. When fully operational, which was expected to be in 2021, Galileo will consist of 24 active satellites with a second generation of satellites to replace older equipment to become operational after 2025.

Russia is building the GLONASS system. Starting in 1982, the system of 24 satellites was in place by 1995. However, difficult economic conditions between 1989 and 1999 caused the funding for space activities to be cut by 80 per cent and Russia could not maintain the full network. Only six operational satellites were in place by 2001. Following an improvement in the economy, President Putin gave high priority to restoring the system, which was back to normal by July 2013. It was planned to improve the system's accuracy to 0.6m or better by 2020 with the latest version satellite design, GLONASS-K2, in service in 2022.

China has had a limited test system of three geostationary satellites called BeiDou-1 operating since 2000 and offering navigational services to users in China and neighbouring regions. The system is named after the Ursa Major constellation which is known in China as Běidǒu. The second-generation system, called BeiDou-2 or Compass, started operating in 2011. BeiDou-2 had five geostationary satellites for backward compatibility with BeiDou-1, 27 in Medium Earth Orbit and three in inclined geosynchronous orbit. The final satellite of the third-generation BeiDou system, BDS-3, went into orbit in June 2020 and will offer global coverage.

India has developed the Indian Regional Navigational Satellite System (IRNSS), which will be under the complete control of the Indian government and will provide coverage of the Indian sub-continent and the Indian Ocean. It consists of eight satellites: three in geostationary orbit and five in inclined geosynchronous orbit. The IRNSS satellite will also carry corner cube reflectors for laser ranging. The final satellite was launched in 2018.

Japan is building a regional system that will augment GPS coverage in Japan. High-rise buildings in Japanese cities give rise to many urban canyons making it difficult to receive GPS signals. The Quasi-Zenith Satellite System (QZSS) in synchronous orbit provides additional signals compatible with GPS. In March 2013, it was announced that the QZSS would be enlarged from three to four satellites and the system became fully operational in 2018. Instead of onboard atomic clocks, Japan is experimenting with quartz clocks that are kept in synchronism with atomic clocks on the ground; this should result in considerable cost savings.

6.18 Space Debris

While artificial satellites have brought great benefits, there are also difficult problems that may constrain future operations in space. Chief of these is the problem of space debris or space junk. There are more than 22,000 pieces of human-generated debris bigger than 10cm being tracked in orbit and an estimated 500,000 pieces as small as one centimetre that are too small to track regularly. With relative velocities of about 10km/s, even these small objects have huge kinetic energy and pose a serious hazard to operational satellites.

Space debris consists of spent rocket stages, old satellites and fragments from disintegrations and collisions. Each time a collision occurs, many smaller pieces are created, thus adding to the problem. Russia is responsible for about 40 per cent of space junk, followed by the US (30 per cent), China

6.23 (left)—Logo of the EU's Galileo GPS.

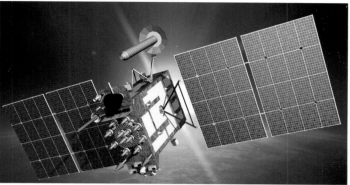

6.24 (above)—Artist's impression of the GLONASS navigation satellite.

6.25 (above)—Logo of the Chinese BeiDou navigation satellite system.

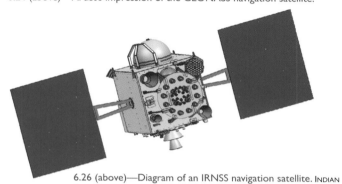

6.26 (above)—Diagram of an IRNSS navigation satellite. INDIAN SPACE RESEARCH ORGANISATION

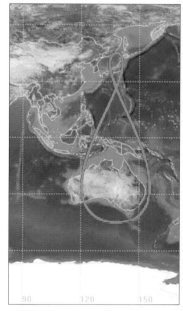

6.27 (above)—Satellite orbit of Japan's QZSS regional satellite GPS augmentation system. CREATIVE COMMONS 3.0

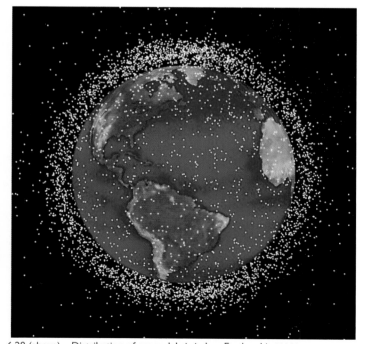

6.28 (above)—Distribution of space debris in low Earth orbit. NASA

(20 per cent) and the rest of the world (10 per cent).

In January 2007, a Chinese weather satellite, Fengyun-1C, with a mass of 750 kg, was deliberately destroyed by a head-on collision as part of an anti-satellite missile test. The collision created more than 2,300 pieces of trackable debris, over 35,000 pieces one centimetre or larger and a million pieces one millimetre or larger. The test took place at 850km altitude, a part of near-Earth space very densely populated by satellites. China was widely condemned for this action both for the military implications as well as the huge amount of debris it created.

The rising amount of space debris increases the danger to all space vehicles but is especially crucial for manned spacecraft such as the ISS. In November 2012, the ISS was boosted one kilometre higher in orbit to avoid a possible collision with a fragment of Iridium-33 that collided with the derelict Cosmos 2251 on 10 February 2009. That had been the fifteenth unscheduled manoeuvre of the ISS in order to avoid debris.

The ground-based radar of the US Space Surveillance Network (known as the Space Fence) tracks objects greater than 10cm and can detect objects as small as three millimetres. In addition, the US Tactical Technology Office has developed an advanced Space Surveillance Telescope that will track fragments optically; it will accurately track objects in geosynchronous orbit and will yield about a terabyte (2^{40} bytes) of data each night it is operating.

Even without any new satellite launches, the existing debris in Low Earth Orbit will continue to grow over the next few decades through collisions. It is generally agreed that it is necessary to remove the largest pieces of space debris in order to mitigate the collisional cascade process. Tackling the space debris problem will require unprecedented international co-operation.

6.29—Part of the US Space Fence system for radar-tracking space debris.

7. The Future

Prediction is very difficult, especially if it is about the future
Neils Bohr (1885–1962)

7.1 Dublin Port Company

Located in the heart of Dublin City and at the hub of the national road and rail network, Dublin port is a key strategic access point for Ireland and in particular the Dublin area. It handles almost 50 per cent of all trade in the Republic of Ireland.

Originally under the Department of Industry and Commerce, the port is now sponsored by the Department of Transport. The port is operated by Dublin Port Company, a semi-state body, which was incorporated on 28 February 1997, replacing the Dublin Port and Docks Board, set up in 1867, and its predecessor, the Ballast Board, set up in 1786. Dublin Port Company is responsible for the management, control, operation and development of the port.

The port is part of the national and global transport system. It is one of five major ports classified

7.01—Dublin Port and Bull Island (top right). Dublin Port Company

as Tier 1 / Tier 2 ports in National Port Policy. In the EU's Trans-European Transport Network (TEN-T) it is categorised as a core / comprehensive port, i.e., a port making the most important connections between transport nodes.

7.02—Logo of the Dublin Port Company.

To provide future national port capacity and play its role in global sea transportation, it must maintain its facilities at the highest possible standard, responding alike to short-term changes arising from economic fluctuations and long-term trends in world shipping. Planning for development involves anticipating not alone future trade volumes but also possible changes in the composition of goods handled, developments in global shipping technology, the after-effects of Brexit, environmental pressures, including possible flooding risk, and the need to meet targets for reduced carbon emissions and environmental sustainability.

These create the impetus to utilise existing resources more efficiently while also putting additional infrastructure in place.

Over centuries, port activity has moved eastward and downriver from the centre of Dublin, putting the port at a distance from city dwellers and the city. Some of the future developments planned by Dublin Port Company will make port activities more integral to the city and facilitate recreational activities within the port.

7.03—Corn Exchange, Burgh Quay and the Customs House in the late 18th century. Shipping and trade have moved downriver from the centre of Dublin. SAMUEL F. BROCAS

DUBLIN CUSTOM HOUSE DOCKS' BONDED WAREHOUSES.   A VISTA IN THE WINE AND SPIRIT VAULTS

This vault is about 474 feet in length by 104 feet in width, and is capable of storing upwards of 20,000 mixed casks. Many of these are maturing in bond for over 16 years. The mean temperature of the vault is from 55° to 60°. When the Irish Free State Government was established, the value of the " wet goods " stored in the eleven bonded warehouses within the Department, including duty, was estimated at about £6,000,000.

7.2 Trade through Dublin Port

The volume and composition of goods traded through Dublin port have reflected the evolution of Ireland's economy over time. In the Viking era, Dublin was part of a trading network that linked Scandinavia, England and Europe and was a centre for the slave trade, which contributed to the early city's economic growth.

In medieval times there was trade in cattle hides to England and Europe with a strong return trade in imported wine, pottery and other goods. The Georgian era, when the city was a centre for administration with an independent parliament, and landowners acquired large town houses in the newly-built streets and squares, saw a strong trade in imported luxury goods for the wealthy classes while linen and agricultural goods were exported.

The city and its port declined following the Act of Union with Britain in 1800 but agricultural goods continued to be exported and coal imported. By the 1800s, most of the trade was to British ports.

As the Irish economy developed in the twentieth century the composition of trade reflected the changes. Export of live cattle was replaced by chilled meat; oil took the place once occupied by coal and today's trade includes the output of the modern digital and technology sector.

7.05—The car carrier
Emden at Dublin Port.
DENIS BERGIN, DUBLIN PORT
ARCHIVE, 2014

7.3 Trade Today

The main activity of the port is handling freight. In 2019, 7,898 ships arrived in port. The overall volume of imports was over 22 million gross tonnes and exports were over 15 million gross tonnes. The bulk of this was carried as unitised trade, chiefly in roll-on roll-of (ro–ro) and lift-on lift-off (lo–lo) units. Next in volume was lo–lo teu cargo (teu is a cargo measurement equivalent to a 20-ft container unit), imports of new trade vehicles and bulk goods in liquid, solid or break bulk form.

The dominance of ro–ro freight as a component of port traffic is expected to continue to 2040, the end year of the current Masterplan for future port development. In addition to ongoing trade between Ireland and Britain, Dublin Port Company anticipates that new ro–ro freight services to the Continent and to Africa will raise ro–ro trade as a proportion of port traffic to 70 per cent, or 41.9 million tonnes, by 2040. The expected volume of lo–lo trade will be 1.1 million teu, or 0.6 million unit loads. Brexit is also changing trade between Ireland and the UK but it is too early to say what changes it will cause.

Providing the increased capacity to handle this level of ro–ro freight will be a key aspect of future infrastructural planning, requiring optimal use of existing land. It is notable that the volume of trade handled by the port has quadrupled in the last 30 years without the addition of any new land in the port area. Sufficient spare capacity already exists, as well as potential to further increase lo–lo throughput by optimising the use of container terminals, to increase container handling capacity to 1.9 million teu per annum on existing port land. The port currently occupies 261 hectares (ha).

Maximising the efficient use of cargo handling space will enable the quick turnaround of ships. Designated cargo handling areas must be close to quay walls as moving cargo from the quays to transit areas is inefficient and delays ship turnaround time.

7.4 World Trade

In order to estimate future demands on Dublin port, it is instructive to look at the recent developments in world trade. According to the United Nations Conference on Trade and Development (UNCTAD) figures for the size of the world fleet between 2005 and 2011, in terms of deadweight, which is the maximum weight a ship can carry including cargo, fuel, freshwater, stores and crew, showed strong growth in the three-year period 2005–07. Then growth paused due to the world recession and was renewed in the period 2009–11 amounting to nearly seven per cent per annum. In 2011, the total worldwide shipping capacity was 8.9 billion tonnes, which is equivalent to 1.27 tonnes for every person on the planet.

—This upward trend in global economic activity was stalled by social and economic lockdowns introduced worldwide in 2020–21 to control rising infections caused by the Covid-19 pandemic. The world economy dropped into recession on a scale of severity equal to the 1930s Great Depression. The 2020 UNCTAD report on world trade warned of a contraction in the global economy of 4.3 per cent in 2020, with a recovery in 2021 dependent on whether further Covid-19 lockdowns were introduced. The volume of international maritime trade was predicted to contract by 4.1 per cent in 2020. The sudden collapse in global demand for goods had a severe impact on the volume of cargo shipped and, hence, on port traffic. Such fluctuations in global economic growth are the unforeseeable changes in circumstances that a port like Dublin must adapt to.

Changes that are possible to anticipate include the trend towards larger container ships. The capacity of the largest container ships rose by 10.9 per cent in 2019. The increased size of container vessels will require ports to change their access and infrastructure if they are to be accommodated. If the size of container ships continues to increase over the time scale of the Masterplan, new, deeper berths may have to be built. A potential location for deeper berths exists beside the ESB power station at Poolbeg. Some degree of reclamation may be required also.

7.06—The ontainer shp *Thea 11* and Dublin Port Co. Pilot. DENIS BERGIN, DUBLIN PORT ARCHIVE, 2014

Growth in the volume of unitised cargo (ro-ro and lo-low) is expected to continue but the volume going to the United Kingdom will fall while the volume carried on ro-ro and lo-lo services to continental Europe will increase. Changes in trading patterns post-Brexit will see new direct shipping routes to continental Europe while facilities for inspection, seal and documentation checks will be located at Dublin port.

Responding appropriately over decades to such short and longer-term developments will require flexibility on the part of port planners and the Masterplan.

7.5 Cruise Liners

Activity in the port is not confined to handling the import and export of traded goods. Tourist traffic is a significant component of port activity, with 1.9 million passengers and 559,506 tourist vehicles using the port in 2019, thus demonstrating the importance of the ferries.

In recent years, Dublin has become a popular destination for cruise liners and visiting cruise ships represent a growing element of port traffic; in 2012 and 2013, there were 85 and 100 respectively. In 2019, 158 cruise calls were made to the port, carrying 323,234 passengers and crew. The average size of ships increased also.

However, the sustainability of this form of tourist traffic is a consideration for Dublin Port Company given the high financial investment required to accommodate cruise vessels and the balance between costs and benefits for the port and the city as a whole. The views of stakeholders on the

7.07—The cruise liner *Nautica*. DENIS BERGIN, DUBLIN PORT ARCHIVE, 2014

7.08—CLdN's *Celine* the world's largest short-sea Ro-Ro vessel, on her maiden voyage, 2017. PADDY MADDOCK

future of cruise tourism for the city and the aim of the Masterplan to socially re-integrate the port with the city will inform future investment decisions.

7.6 Ferry Services

Irish Ferries operates two ships from the passenger terminal at the east end of the North Wall. The MV *Ulysses*, built in 2001, is the largest ferry in the world in terms of its vehicle capacity. It can carry 2000 passengers, 1342 cars and 240 trucks and takes a little over three hours for the crossing to Holyhead. The MV *Jonathan Swift* is a high-speed catamaran ferry, which takes less than two hours to cross to Holyhead. It can carry 800 passengers and 200 cars. A third ferry, MV *Stena Adventurer*, which also serves Holyhead, is operated by Stena Lines. It was launched in 2003 and can accommodate 1500 passengers and 640 cars. There is considerable rivalry between the two shipping firms and Stena like to point out that their MV *Adventurer* is three metres longer than the MV *Ulysses*; it also stands higher above the waterline.

The P&O Line operates three conventional ferries, MVs *Norbay*, *Norbank* and *European Endeavour*, on the Liverpool crossing. There are 20 sailings per week, each taking seven and a half hours.

7.7 Dublin Port Company Masterplan 2012–2040

On 27 February 2012, Dublin Port Company launched a Masterplan to guide its development over the coming 30 years. At the core of the Masterplan is a list of 14 possible options for the development of the port. The Masterplan was launched by Leo Varadkar, TD, in his capacity as Minister for Transport, Tourism and Sport, who said:

As Ireland's most important port, Dublin port is a vital part of our national infrastructure. It has a significant role to play in growing exports, growing jobs and also in growing tourism, with 87 cruise ships calling last year. This Masterplan follows a detailed consultation process and will ensure that Dublin port continues to make a real contribution to the local economy, and to our export-led recovery.

Eamonn O'Reilly, Chief Executive of Dublin Port Company, commented:
We now handle € 35 billion per annum in trade going in and out of the port and will easily double our volumes by 2040. We need to grow, in a way which better integrates the port with the city and which contributes substantially to improve both the natural and built environments. However, how we do all of this needs to be tempered and modulated by the needs of the city and its citizens.

Although trade by volume through Dublin Port will grow in the coming decades, the source and destination of goods will change as the economy continues to adapt and evolve in response to Brexit. Trade with the UK before Brexit accounted for two-thirds of volume but by 2021 trade coming into Dublin was divided equally between the UK and EU. Since Brexit has become a reality, Ireland has pivoted to focus on trade with continental Europe. Post-Brexit checks on goods are diverting exports that traditionally would have gone through the UK on to other routes. Now, exports travel directly from Dublin to EU ports. In this scenario, the Rotterdam route has become more important than ever. Rotterdam is the largest sea-port in Europe and has excellent accessibility thanks to its geographical position. In response to these new circumstances, freight companies such as CLdN have expanded their Irish service, maximising equipment turnaround and strengthening trade with the Continent.

7.8 Culture and recreation

Port and city reintegration is one of the key policy drivers for Dublin port. For centuries, port activities were ingrained in Dublin's daily life. Ships and the plethora of cargoes they carried flooded the quays of the Liffey. Containerization changed that picture for ever. Since the 1970s, the port has become estranged from the city, confined to the Liffey mouth. Culture and heritage are essential in restoring the relationship between Dublin and its port, providing citizens with new spaces to explore and reconnect with the past and with the port's culture and identity. With that vision in mind, Dublin Port Company is creating a distributed museum on its lands in Dublin city.

Odlums Mill, a six-storey concrete grain silo built in the 1920s in the Alexandra Basin in the port area north of the Liffey, will be the central element of the distributed museum and the future heritage plans for the port. It is to be transformed into a cultural hub in the heart of the industrial port, housing a port museum and archive, a theatre, studios for artists, community rooms and some port operations relocated from other areas of the port. The masterplan for the Odlums Mill site includes the construction of a 900-metre elevated walkway bringing visitors from the 3Arena to the Mill cultural centre, giving walkers views over the working port area on the way.

Close to Odlums is The Pumphouse heritage zone, in the former Graving Docks premises. It opened its door to the public in 2021 hosting theatre performances such as the *Book of Names*, *Canaries* and *Outrage*. It will be expanded in a subsequent phase to incorporate the Victorian Graving Dock No. 1, which will be excavated and revealed.

Another historical landmark being redeveloped is the Victorian red-brick substation at the junction of Alexandra Road and East Wall Road. It was included in the Record of Protected Structures and the port is restoring and redeveloping the space to turn it into a visitor centre.

A second major element of the Masterplan, which will open up access to the port from the city, is a new recreational greenway stretching over three kilometres from Bond Road to Alexandra Road Extension, with a park at Alexandra Road Extension, observation points and extensive landscaping.

The greenway and distributed museum landmarks will link through different pedestrian and

7.10—The revived Liffey Ferry approaches the Diving Bell, the start point for the port's distributed museum. DUBLIN PORT COMPANY

cycling routes. The distributed museum starts at the Diving Bell (restored in 2015 and turned into Ireland's smallest museum) and, throughout 6.3km, will give Dubliners a real sense of the city, the port and the bay.

7.9 Environment and wildlife

Dublin Port Company's commitment to biodiversity and sustainability means ensuring the port can operate to meet present and future human needs while preserving the environment and supporting the implementation of the National Biodiversity Action Plan, thereby continuing to operate sustainably into the future.

Dublin Bay is a UNESCO Biosphere, a world designated site for testing and reconciling sustainable human activity with the conservation of biodiversity. Stretching from Howth to Killiney, it is the only biosphere worldwide that includes a capital city within its area.

Bull Island is an important part of Dublin Biosphere. The construction of the Great North Wall between 1821 and 1824 had the happy effect of creating the five-kilometre Bull Island from sand that built up on the seaward side of the wall. The members of the Ballast Board would have been gratified to know that their project had such a beneficial outcome for the citizens of Dublin.

In 1962–4, Dublin Corporation built a causeway from the coast road to a point about half way along the island to give easier access and, from 1986, an interpretive centre has provided visitors with information about the flora and fauna.

7.11—Bull Island accommodates human activity and rich biodiversity. DUBLIN PORT COMPANY / WILLIAM MURPHY

In September 2013, Dublin Port Company announced a proposal to transfer its ownership of a significant portion of Bull Island to Dublin City Council to hold in perpetuity for the people of Dublin. The Company will collaborate with the Council and Fáilte Ireland to produce a feasibility study for a new interpretative centre on Bull Island and will contribute to the development of a masterplan for the UNESCO biosphere reserve. It will allocate up to €1.2 million towards the cost of the study, the masterplan and new services or facilities identified for the island.

Bull Island offers a variety of habitats for wildlife, which include intertidal mudflats, salt marsh, freshwater marsh, dunes and a beach area. It was designated a bird sanctuary in 1931, a UNESCO biosphere in 1981 and a national nature reserve in 1988. The mudflats support a large population of birds and at any time up to 27,000 birds are present, which gives the area the highest bird density in Ireland. Many of the birds are migratory and these wildfowl and waders visit the island in such numbers that they give the island an international significance. Bird species on the island include brent geese, curlews, oystercatchers, grey plovers, northern shovelers, little egrets, reed buntings and little terns. The mammal species on the island include brown rats, red foxes, field mice, Irish hares, hedgehogs and rabbits. Common seals and grey seals are also found in the surrounding waters and can be seen regularly hauled out on sand at low tide at the tip of the island near Howth. The fresh water marsh is important for its wealth of wild flowers, particularly orchids.

BirdWatch Ireland and Dublin Port Company have combined forces to learn more about how waterbirds use Dublin Bay. The Company has supported a comprehensive programme of bird counts within the bay to identify the most important areas used by the birds. A programme to ring wader species will bring a better understanding of the habits of oystercatchers, redshanks and bar-tailed godwits and will guide measures to reduce the impact of disturbance, development and climate change.

7.12—Terns migrate to Dublin port from West Africa. MARTA LOPEZ ALARCÓN

The tern colonies

The Liffey within the port area is home to a growing colony of terns, which migrate from as far away as West Africa. Birdwatch Ireland reported that in 2011 the colonies had 499 breeding pairs of common tern and 37 pairs of arctic tern; well over 700 chicks were ringed. Dublin Port Company supplied floating platforms for the terns. The development of new quays on the south bank of the river will require the relocation of the two tern colonies from the mooring dolphins they occupy alongside the shipping channel. It is proposed to relocate the tern colonies to sites north of the eastern ferry terminal.

7.10 The Dublin Array

There is a proposal to build a large windfarm called the Dublin Array in the southern approaches of Dublin Bay. It will be situated about 10 kilometres offshore on the Kish and Bray sandbanks and will extend about three kilometres in the east–west direction and about 18 kilometres in the north–south direction, giving an overall area of about 54 sq. kilometres. It will be comparable in size with the first phase of the London Array.

The Array will consist of up to 145 offshore turbines each with an installed capacity in the range three to six megawatts depending on when they are installed. The turbine heights will be between 85 and 100 metres above sea level with a total height of no more than 160 metres.

The wind turbines will be supported on a foundation of a steel monopile and a transition piece. A monopile is a long cylindrical steel tube with a diameter from 4.0 to 6.5 metres and it is installed on the seabed to a depth of between 20 and 40 metres by a special purpose rig. It may be necessary to remove rocks or other obstructions to place the monopile correctly. The monopile is capped with

7.13—Site and distribution of the Dublin Array offshore windfarm.

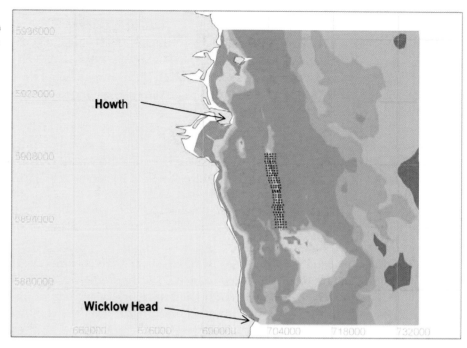

7.14—XOCEAN XO-450 Uncrewed Surface Vessel (USV) at Sea Surveying Offshore Windfarm.

a transition piece, which has ladders and platforms for access. The turbine tower will be bolted onto a flange on top of the transition piece.

The turbines will be connected in groups by low-voltage cables in trenches and brought to an offshore substation located near the centre of the array. The voltage will be increased at the substation for transmission along a high-voltage cable to the shore at Shanganagh, about two kilometres north of Bray. The connection to the national grid will be completed by an underground cable to the ESB substation at Carrickmines.

The promoters propose that the electrical energy will either be used in Ireland or exported to the UK in accord with the agreement between the Irish and UK governments allowing trading in renewables. During construction the promoters envisage leasing space from Dublin port to facilitate construction. It is estimated that the total capital cost of the project will be in the region of €2 billion.

Coda

We live in an ever-changing world where old technologies are replaced by new ones and good theories are replaced by better ones. Our quality of life depends on choosing the most appropriate technologies for our time and on having the flexibility to adapt to new ways of doing things. This requires educational systems that are both broad and deep so that lifelong learning becomes the norm. The future will always surprise us and we must be prepared to cope with whatever it throws at us.

7.15—The port maritime sculpture garden with the 'Drop' sculpture by Eimear Murphy in the foreground. WILLIAM MURPHY, CREATIVE COMMONS 2.0

Appendices

APPENDIX I

THE
DUBLIN PENNY JOURNAL

CONDUCTED BY P. DIXON HARDY, M.R.I.A.
Vol. II.   AUGUST 15, 1835 No. 163..R.I.A.

A STORY OF THE LAST CENTURY

The improvements made in the harbour of Dublin, within the last sixty years, (or thereabouts,) cannot fail to fill the beholder with admiration. Every way the eye turns the taste and spirit of our fellow-citizens are displayed—beauty is combined with utility. The feeble citizen of fourscore, as he saunters along the quay of the north or south wall, recalls to his memory, that in his boyhood those beautiful walks which he now enjoys were swampy impossible strands–that from Ballybough to Ball's Bridge, and from Mark's Church to Ringsend, were under the dominion of the waves of the Atlantic. Ringsend might then be deemed an island, for, before the Dodder River was enclosed by banks, the sea rolled over where rich pastures now relieve the eye in the vicinity of Irishtown; though it is to be regretted, that of all places round the harbour Ringsend is the least improved–it is, in fact disgusting in its appearance, while some of its ruinous buildings seem to threaten destruction to the unwary passenger.

In this place there is, fit present, living, an individual who has resided there nearly a century—who remembers the situation of the harbour upwards of seventy years ago—and who gives the following account of the origin of Ringsend and the Pidgeon House. Speaking on the subject some short time since, he observed–"I well remember the harbour of Dublin destitute of a light house, save one on Howth. Vessels of all burden were obliged to remain beyond the bar after nightfall, owing to the vast shoal shore lying north and south, called the north and south bulls. When they entered the harbour, the first place of security they met was Ringsend, so called from many score rings of a prodigious size fastened in beams of wood, protruding from this neck of land; other rings made fast in enormous rocks, brought for that purpose, the bottom being too soft for anchorage. Thus, from the end of land with rings, it was called in time Ringsend; its original name I leave to the antiquarian to discover. A wall was then begun by the Corporation of the city, where the Pidgeon House now stands, to make some shelter for the shipping; but this did not, in the least, remedy the danger. A wall farther out was con- sidered indispensable; piles were sunk for the under-taking, and a wooden house, strongly cramped with iron, to serve as a watch-house, store-house, find place of refuge for any that might be forced there through stress of weather.

Large sums of money were collected from the citizens by the Corporation; –the work went on with spirit for about two years, then all on a sudden it stopped, and remained so for a long time, until the Ballast Office Company was established, who took it on themselves to finish it. To return to the building of the old wall, as it is now called ; there were a number of boats plying from Ringsend to the pile-ends, where the new wall to the Light House commences, and which by many is called the Pile-ends to thia day, and not without cause, for still the piles or stakes are to be been. In those days the Black Rock, or clean kitchen of Dunleary, was not heard of. During the time the works were going on, the word was, of a Sunday–'Where shall we go?' 'To the Pile-ends, and take our dinner in Pidgeon s house;'–alluding to a man that lived in a large wooden house, as before described, at the Pile-ends. This man was left in care of the workmen's tools and works. He had one son, two daughters, and wife. Pidgeon finding the great resort to his house in the summer, spared no expense to make it neat for their reception;–had bottled ale, and several other kinds of drink, for public accommodation, He next fitted out a boat, in a tasteful style, which himself and son rowed. He plied none but the most respectable companies of which he had a great resort.

From this man the Pidgeon House took its name, though some will have it that from a battery that was afterwards built of an hectangular form with loop-holes which, to all appearance, represented, at a distance a pidgeon house, such as we see in some of our farm-yards, elevated on poles; while others affirm that from the carrier pidgeons resting here it took its name; but alt the old inhabitants of Dublin and Ringsend contend for the first.

It may be interesting to the reader to follow up the history of Pidgeon and his family.

For two summers Pidgeon was doing well, having a yearly salary for minding the works. One night, however, four men came under the window in a boat and pleaded distress–they got admission, bin as soon as they regaled themselves all started up, every man with a sabre in his hand, and seizing the old couple, tied them back to back, The young man (Ned Pidgeon) snatched a hand-spike, and courageously attacked them; but, unfortunately, one of the ruffians directed a deadly blow at his sister, which he prevented by seizing the sword, which the ruffian drew through his hand, and cut some arteries that disabled him for life. However, in this wounded state be fled to another hut, lately built, to call the as-stance of two men who lived in it, but, in his short absence, the ruffians plundered the place of every valuable article they could lay hands on, and would have put the old couple to death were it not for the tears of the two girls. Ruffians as they were, they paid regard to their intreaties and offered them no improper violence, save pulling a ring from one of their fingers.

Ned Pidgeon returned with the two men, and was overjoyed to find all alive–and might have been in time to prevent the robbery was it not for the dressing that his hand required, which was done in a hasty man- ner. Finding the robbers gone, he ran out with the two men, who had each a brace of large pistols, and himself a smaller one, in order to make chase; but when they got down to the boats, they found them disabled, by means of boat-hooks driven, in many parts, through them, and they filled with water; so they were obliged to return. Pidgeon's boat, in particular, was stoved to pieces.

The whole family now sat bewailing their losses, except, at intervals, the old man would raise his eyes to heaven, and thank Divine Providence for having preserved their lives.

This afflicting circumstance took place on a Saturday night. The next day some of the citizens, who used to resort to Pidgeon's, were alarmed as well as disappointed by not finding his boat as usual in waiting; however, they too soon were acquainted of the sad affair. Boats were hired at Ringsend, and soon a crowd assembled at the Pile-ends–every one sympathised in poor Pidgeon's distress. As the heart of an Irishman is ever open to feel for the misery of others, his eye swims with tears of joy as he opens his purse to relieve it. A collection was instantaneously set on foot, and as much as might serve his immediate wants presented him. Against the following Sunday he had another boat in readiness, when ano-thcr sum was given him, which nearly made up his losses.

His poor son, Ned, was no more able to pull an oar; however, with one hand he kept the tiller. A few days after the outrage, as himself and his father were out some short distance catching fish for dinner, the old man's hooks fastened in something at the bottom, which, by a gentle pull of his line, seemed to yield to him. His first conjecture was, that it might be a piece of a thick rope, so be drew in the line with caution least he would break his hooks–but mark his terror when the face of a man appeared under the surface of the water. The moment Ned saw it, he exclaimed, with horror in his countenance, yet mingled with marks of exulting joy–'O, father, father, that's one of the villians who robbed us–O yes, yes, father, and the very wretch that disabled me'.

Poor old Pidgeon looked as terrified at the body as if the act was (to be performed over again, and was about to let it go, when Ned reminded him that some of his property might be found about him, but when they towed it to shore they found nothing, save an old silver-cased watch that hung over Pidgeon's fire-place. In a few days more another body was washed upon shore, which proved that the boat had been upset, and that the vengeance of heaven paid them the wages they so justly deserved.

The following winter old Pidgeon died, leaving two daughters, a disabled son, and a poor old helpless wife. By the kindness of the commissioners they were allowed to retain the house, but having no one to row the boat, they had to hire two men, while Ned managed the tiller and received the money from the passengers.

It happened one day, while he was ashore, that one of those oarsmen drew out some cold meat and bread for his dinner, forgetting to lake up the knife with which he cut it from off the seat, Ned, stepping into the boat, saw it, and exclaimed—'Good heavens!' snatching it up as he spoke 'how came my father's pearl-handled Jack o'-the-leg here—the very knife he was robbed of last season.' As he said this he looked, with frantic stare, at the two men, one of them immediately betrayed symptoms of guilt, and with a volley of curses, exclaimed—Do ye think there's no more knives in the world of the same sort'

'Oh, then,' replied Ned, It was in your possession, I see.'

'Aye, that it was.' said the other, 'and shall be there again.'

'Well, then," roared Neil, ' I claim it as my property,! and you are my prisoner,' holding it to the fellow's breast —' stir one inch till we get to shore and you meet your fate.'

Fortunately for Ned, the other boatman had a falling out with this fellow, and would be glad to see him put out of Pidgeon's employment. Ned ordered the boat to where the military were stationed, and just at they approached the landing-place, the fellow made a sudden spring and thought to have snatched the knife out of his hand, but he was on his guard, and made a thrust at him, which to avoid the fellow leaped over board; on rising to the surface of the water his hat fell off and exposed a large wen [swelling] on his head, that convinced Ned he was one of the ruffians who plundered his father on the night referred to.

Ned had him now fully in his power, as the

fellow had on a large pea jacket, which prevented him swimming. Fixing a noose to a line, he threw it over him, and caught him by the wrist, and then fastened it to the stern of the boat in such a manner that he could not extricate himself. He was brought immediately a prisoner into Dublin;—Ned swore to his knife and his person;—he was sentenced to die. In prison he confessed the whole affair, viz.—a dispute arising in the boat, at the dividing; of the booty, himself and another of the gang threw the other two over board. After committing this horrible act he had a similar quarrel with the other fellow, who, in the heat of his wrath, threatened to inform when he would get ashore. 'This so enraged me,' said the prisoner, 'that I snatched up that very knife that discovered me, and stabbed him, and threw him overboard. The unfortunate wretch rose over water, screeching and seizing the gunnel, endeavouring to get in again, when turning to the same side to shove him off, a wave came and upset the boat—I saw him no more. The keel of the boat showed uppermost, which I mounted, still holding the knife; there I sat until day was breaking, when I was picked up by a smuggler, who supposed all came by accident; she continued her voyage, and I was held by my policy in great trust: we made three voyages. One right, while landing some hogsheads of tobacco in the dark, my foot came between two of them which so disabled me that the crew carried me to another part of the coast, and there left me ashore, that there might be time enough to convey the goods out of sight, least when I'd recover, I might inform. There I was left on the shore, far away from any house or hut, which, indeed, was too good for such a wretch. With all the horrors of a guilty mind, and the screams of the wretch that I stabbed in my ears. I was about to end my existence with that very same knife, when an old man arrested my arm and brought me to his

cabin. I soon got well but unfitted any longer for sea, was obliged to turn myself to rowing a ferry boat, until hired by Pidgeon. I cannot tell the reason why I kept the bloody knife, often was going to throw it into the sea, but something always prevented me.'

Soon after the execution of this fellow, Ned Pidgeon complained of a pain in his disabled hand—a visible sore appeared: at last a mortification set in. In spite of all medicine or ointment it spread — amputation was the only remedy to save his life, but, alas, it had not this effect, for the poor fellow died in the operation.

The two poor girls, Mary and Rachel, were now left without any human being to protect them save a poor feeble mother who only survived her son six weeks.— 'Tis true that their boat was plying, but they did not receive from the fellows that rowed it one-third of the money, besides they were rude and uncivil to their passengers, which made many that used to frequent Pidgeon's house, withdraw their visits.

In this uncomfortable state they consulted each other on what plan they could procure a livelihood.

They were about to sell the boat and go into town, but what could they do there? They were as great strangers to the land as the fish of the sea.

At last it was agreed, that as they had learned to handle the oar in amusement on fishing excursions with their father, they might now turn it to advantage, as it would be a novelty, and excite the pity of the citizens by seeing two tolerably handsome females manage a boat, which they could do well. Their design had the desired effect. The boat was newly painted—a suitable and yet becoming dress made for the fair mariners — in a short time their boat was more frequented than ever— men of all ages and rank were contending for the oars, nor were they allowed, except on some extraordinary occasion to give a pull.

8.01—A wooden watchhouse built near Ringsend housed the watchman John Pidgeon, who gave his name to the area.

It chanced about the beginning of October, that a very respectable party visited Pidgeon's. The two girls threw off their amphibious costume and appeared in their gayest attire to wait upon them, which they did in a most graceful way. The company had their own boat in waiting, which made them indulge their delay later than they otherwise would have done. Having at length taken their departure, Mary and her sister sat down to to take some refreshment, when, all of a sudden a violent storm arose. By and bye they hear a gun of distress: every candle that their small windows could hold were lighted to serve as a beacon for such as might escape the fury of the storm. Three long hours they sat expecting every moment to he called on to administer comfort to some exhausted being. About midnight the storm died away, and the sky became lightsome. Mary went to the door to look over the sea. when calling to Rachel she said I see something black, do you Rachel? 1 think it a boat at no great distance—Oh I shudder for the people that

were with us to-day.' 'Where do you see it' replied Rachel—' oh aye, I see it now—I think it more like a barrel.' 'No Rachel,' said Mary, 'I think not, fetch me the glass'. The glass was brought, when she exclaimed 'Oh! Rachel, Rachel, I see a man on a plank, the sea is not too rough–out with the boat, out with the boat.'

Their light pliant oars were soon put in motion with more than usual exertion. Their little boat, skipping from wave to wave, soon reached the plank, where they found two men and a child, one of them lying on the broad of back almost exhausted, and the child on his breast, while his feeble and wearied hands endeavoured to keep its little head erect, as now and then a light wave broke over them. The other man sat astride, keeping his feet in motion in the nature of paddles.

The boat soon came up with them, but so exhausted were the men that they had lost all power of speech. The child was the first relieved from danger, next the two men were placed at the stern text of the boot by the intrepidity of those courageous girls; and, after about twenty minutes rowing, were landed, and safely conveyed to the warm shelter of Pidgeon's house—put into warm beds, and some warm drink administered, which soon threw them into a sound sleep. The child (a fine boy of five years old} was looked to with still greater care, as its age demanded.

When morning broke, the two girls went out to see from what wreck they had escaped, when by the assistance of their telescope, they discovered two vessels on the north bull; one seemed to have received little damage save to her rigging, but the other suffered much. The strangers now awake, and scarcely could persuade themselves but that they were brought there by something supernatural. However they were soon convinced to the contrary; their fair deliverers paid them a visit, and brought to their bedside a suitable breakfast. The man before described as paddling with his feet on the plank was master of one of the vessels from New York, the other, a gentleman passenger whose wife had died in America when the child was but one year old, and was coming to Ireland to place it under the care of some of his wife's relations.

The master of the vessel soon found himself strong enough to look after his wrecked vessel, but the gentleman, having three of his ribs broken, was confined to his bed. Medical men were sent for who declared that if he were moved from where he lay it would be dangerous, so he composed his mind to remain under the care of his deliverers.

In a few days he got an account that almost all of his property was saved from the wreck, which with the thoughts of his child being safe, in some degree alleviated the pain of his mind and body; and under the care of Mary

Pidgeon he speedily recovered. Everything she gave him seemed to possess a charm; his child clung to her wherever she moved, and the stranger looked on Mary with more than ordinary affection.

Being perfectly recovered he presented her with three score pounds, and was about to bid her a long adieu but neither coaxing or threatening could induce the child to part with Mary—so great was the attachment he had formed for her. The stranger now altered his mind with respect to leaving his son in Ireland, so bidding Mary farewell, went to see relations who lived about sixty miles from Dublin, and left hit son in her care till his return.

In about a month he came back, and if his son loved Mary, he himself appeared to have caught the pleasing infection to a greater degree. He found it as great a difficulty to leave her as to get his son away; so to set all at rest, he took lodgings in town, and had the ever binding seal of matrimony impressed on her. He also promised Rachel a good husband as soon as they would reach America; so purchasing some merchandise he embarked with a larger family than he had brought with him. On his arrival he was as good as his word, Rachel was married to a very respectable man in trade.

After they left the pile ends a stone house was erected on the spot, which remains to this day and has been ever since a kind of hotel, and place of refreshment for people in stress of weather, but since the new harbour in Kingstown, has been finished, and steam navigation becomes so general, it has been shut up, as no vessel now puts into Pidgeon House. **T.E.**

APPENDIX 2

Engineers of Dublin Port and their dates in office

Francis Tunstall	1786–1800	Inspector of Works
George Halpin Senior	1800–1854	Inspector of Works
George Halpin Junior	1854–1862	Inspector of Works
Dr Bindon Blood Stoney FRS	1862–1898	Engineer in Chief
Sir John Purser Griffith FRS	1898–1913	Engineer in Chief
Joseph H. Mallagh	1917–1941	Engineer in Chief
F.W. Bond	1942–1953	Engineer in Chief
C.J. Buckley	1953–1965	Engineer in Chief
Paul O'Sullivan	1965–1974	Engineer in Chief
M.C. Smyth	1974–2015	Engineer in Chief

8.02—George Halpin jnr, the third Inspector of Works at Dublin port.

APPENDIX 3

Observing Assistants at Birr Castle, 1848–1916

Lord Rosse's 72-inch reflecting telescope at Parsonstown (Birr)

William Parsons, 3rd Earl of Rosse, completed his great 72-inch reflecting telescope – *The Leviathan* – in February 1845. In autumn 1845, observational work was brought to a halt by the failure of the Irish potato crop and the resulting Great Famine. The Earl and Countess of Rosse devoted all their time and most of their income to alleviating the terrible effects of the famine.

By 1847, when observations were resumed, there were many other demands on the Earl's time so he asked Romney Robinson, director of Armagh Observatory, to suggest a suitable person to make observations when he was absent. Robinson suggested his nephew, **William Hautenville Rambaut** (1822–93), and instructed him in the use of the telescopes at the end of autumn 1847. Rambaut was the first of a succession of able assistants, many of whom went on to have distinguished careers. On gaining his degree from Trinity in the spring of 1848, Rambaut left to become his uncle's second assistant in Armagh. Rambaut contributed to the Armagh Catalogue of 5,345 stars, which earned Robinson the Royal Medal of the Royal Society. He was ordained a priest in the Church of Ireland in 1861 and served as curate and rector in several parishes.

George Johnstone Stoney (1826–1911) was appointed in July 1848. He not only used the 72-inch telescope but also taught Parsons' eldest son, seven-year-old Laurence. Lord Rosse was particularly interested in the Whirlpool Nebula, and Stoney measured the relative positions of 78 of its foreground stars with a micrometer, an astronomical instrument for measuring very small angles or distances. On one night in March 1850, he was rewarded with the discovery of 12 galaxies in the constellation Lynx. Stoney left in June 1850 when he returned to Trinity to compete for Fellowship and his brother Bindon took his place. George Stoney was not successful in competing for Fellowship, receiving the second Madden prize in 1851 and the first in 1852. Lord Rosse supported his application for the chair of Natural Philosophy in Queen's College, Galway, which he held from 1852 to 1857 and during which time he often stayed at Birr Castle. G.J. Stoney's subsequent career is described in Appendix 5.

Bindon Blood Stoney (1829–1909) took over from his older brother George, staying from July 1850 until September 1852. Bindon was a very productive observer and in 26 months he discovered no fewer than 91 new objects. He was mainly concerned with studying the spiral structure of galaxies. Of particular note was his sketch of the central region of the Orion Nebula known as the Trapezium. When a discrepancy of two degrees in the positions of some stars was reported by M.O. Struve of Pulkova Observatory, Bindon tracked down the source of the error to the construction of the universal joint that supported the telescope. He was able to apply appropriate corrections to previous observations. During autumn 1850 and spring 1851, George often joined Bindon at weekends and they observed together.

In December 1853, **Robert J. Mitchell** was engaged to work as observer and tutor of the Parsons' sons. He may have been the Robert J. Mitchell who graduated from The Queen's University of Ireland with a B.A. in 1854 and an M.A. in 1860. Mitchell left Birr Castle to take up a position as inspector of National Schools.

Thomas T. Gray, who was a tutor, later became a Senior Fellow and Vice-Provost of TCD from 1916 until his death in 1924.

Another tutor was **John Purser**, son of John 'Tertius' Purser of Rathmines Castle who effectively ran the Guinness brewery in the 1870s. John Purser held the chair of mathematics in Queen's College, Belfast, from 1863 to 1909 and was highly regarded by his students. His brother Frederick was University Professor of Mathematics in TCD from 1902 to 1909.

Lord Rosse had a high opinion of the ability of his observers and was not slow to acknowledge their diligence:

> I refer with as much confidence to the observations of the two Mr. Stoneys and Mr. Mitchell as if I had on every occasion been present myself, because I know that they had thoroughly mastered the instrument and the methods of observing before they recorded a single independent observation; they were, besides, eminently cautious and painstaking. … Though so many of the observations were made in my absence, they are not the less to be relied on: nothing was done by an unpractised hand, and no pains were spared to ensure accuracy.

The next observer was **Samuel Hunter** who was a graduate of the Dublin School of Design. His main task was to make detailed drawings of the inner part of the Orion Nebula, which had previously been observed by Bindon Stoney. Hunter had to resign in May 1864 due to ill-health.

When William Parsons reached the age of 64, he placed control of the observatory in the hands of his son, Laurence, and he asked **Robert Stawell Ball** (1840–1913) to be tutor to his three younger sons. Ball said he would accept the post, provided he was allowed to use the great telescope. Lord Rosse was happy with this proposal, and appointed him in November 1865, thus giving him free run of the observatory. Ball was a very enthusiastic user of the Leviathan and earned the reputation from the men who worked the telescope of keeping them up 'terrible late' at night. Ball left Birr Castle in August 1867 to take up the chair of Applied Mathematics in the newly established Royal College of Science in Dublin. In 1874, he was appointed Andrews Professor of Astronomy at Dunsink Observatory where he pursued a programme to measure stellar parallax and the orbits of binary stars. He became an accomplished public speaker and undertook three lecture tours of the United States and Canada. In addition, he published over a dozen popular books on astronomy. In 1892, he was appointed to the Lowndean chair of Astronomy and Geometry at Cambridge where he remained until his death in 1913. Ball was elected a Fellow of the Royal Society in 1873 and was knighted in 1886.

William Parsons died on 31 October 1867 and his son **Laurence** assumed the title of 4th Earl of Rosse. He appointed **Charles Edward Burton** (1840–1882) as assistant from February 1868. Burton contributed about 50 observations of nebulae and became proficient in mirror grinding. His silver-on-glass mirrors ranging from six to 15 inches in diameter were said to be unsurpassed. Ill-health forced Burton to resign in March 1869 so he spent some months at his home in Rathmichael, Co. Dublin, where he devoted himself to planetary observations and astronomical photography. In 1870, Burton was well enough to take part in the total solar eclipse expedition to Agosta in Sicily on 22 December and he reported his observations of the corona to the Royal Irish Academy. In 1874, he took part in the expedition to Rodriguez to observe the transit of Venus and he assisted in the reduction of the observations at the Royal Greenwich Observatory. Burton was appointed assistant at Dunsink in 1876 and carried out meticulous transit observations but had to resign in 1878 for health reasons. In the remaining four years of his short life, he continued to make planetary observations and to contribute papers. He was elected a member of the Royal Irish Academy in 1878.

After a gap of almost two years without an assistant, **Ralph Copeland** (1837–1905) was appointed. A trained astronomer who had studied at the University of Göttingen, he started his job in January 1871 and soon made important observations with the 72-inch. Copeland not only revisited known objects like the Andromeda Nebula but also discovered many new nebulae, among them the famous Copeland Septet, a compact group of galaxies in Leo. Copeland resigned in May 1874 to become Ball's assistant at Dunsink until early 1876. He was appointed director of the Earl of Crawford's observatory at Dun Echt in Aberdeenshire and observed the transits of Venus in Mauritius in 1874 and in Jamaica in 1882. He was appointed third Astronomer Royal for Scotland in 1889 and had the task of selecting a new observatory site at Blackford Hill in Edinburgh. Although he travelled abroad to observe total solar eclipses in 1896, 1898 and 1900, his health deteriorated and he died in 1905.

In 1874 the 22-year-old **John Louis Emil Dreyer** (1852–1926) was appointed assistant at Birr. From the age of 14 he had shown a great interest in astronomy and was encouraged by the astronomers in Copenhagen Observatory. Dreyer used both the 36-inch and the 72-inch reflectors to observe star clusters and nebulae. He presented the Royal Irish Academy with an important paper

on additions and corrections to John Herschel's *General Catalogue of Nebulae and Clusters.* In 1878, Dreyer was appointed assistant at Dunsink Observatory and he measured the positions of 321 red stars with the Pistor and Martins Circle. In 1882, at the age of 30, he gained his PhD and was appointed director of Armagh Observatory in succession to Robinson. In 1888, Dreyer published a New General Catalogue of Nebulae that gave the positions and descriptions for 7,840 nebulae. It remains the standard reference used by astronomers the world over and is the origin of the NGC assignation. In 1890, Dreyer published a biography of his countryman Tyco Brahe. Dreyer moved to Oxford in 1916 to pursue his interest in the history of astronomy. He was awarded the Gold Medal of the Royal Astronomical Society in 1916 and served as the society's president from 1923 until 1925. He died in 1926.

The last assistant at Birr was **Otto Boeddicker** (1853–1937) who helped the 4th Earl in his final measurements of the temperature of the lunar surface. From 1868 the modified 36-inch reflector was used with infrared detectors. In 1905, Parsons constructed a special instrument equipped with a short-focus searchlight mirror 24 inches in diameter. His final estimate of the lunar surface temperature was 197° F (75°C). It was always a source of regret to the 4th Earl that his contemporaries did not fully appreciate this achievement. Boeddicker's main objective was to make naked-eye drawings of the Milky Way, which were presented to the Royal Astronomical Society. In February 1916, Boeddicker, as an enemy alien, had to return to Germany. He died in 1937.

Otto Boeddiker (centre) with some of the estate workmen

APPENDIX 4

The Andrews Professors of Astronomy and their dates in office

The Revd Dr Henry Ussher	1783–1790 (below left)
The Revd Dr John Brinkley	1790–1826
Sir William Rowan Hamilton	1827–1865
Dr Franz Friedrich Brünnow	1865–1874
Sir Robert Stawell Ball	1874–1892
Dr Arthur Alcock Rambaut	1892–1897
Dr Charles Jasper Joly	1897–1906
Sir Edmund Taylor Whittaker	1906–1912
Dr Henry Crozier Plummer	1912–1921 (below right)

APPENDIX 5

The Remarkable Stoneys

A5.1 The origin of the Stoneys

We have seen in Chapter 1 the great improvements that Bindon Blood Stoney achieved in Dublin port. Bindon had four close relatives who were equally brilliant in science and engineering – his brother **George Johnstone Stoney** and his nephews **George Gerard Stoney, George Francis FitzGerald** and **Maurice Frederick FitzGerald**. We will also look at another branch of the Stoneys that produced several talented engineers and a mathematical genius.

The Irish Stoneys came from Kettlewell on the River Wharfe in North Yorkshire. The Stoneys were originally Danish and had lived in Yorkshire for over 200 years. On 6 January 1675 (OS or old-style dating before the introduction of the Gregorian calendar), George Stoney of Kettlewell married Mary Moorhouse. Between 1676 and 1691, George and Mary had nine children – six boys and three girls – but only five of the boys survived infancy. After the Glorious Revolution of 1688, George and Mary took advantage of William III's inducement to English Protestants to settle in Ireland. The Stoneys sold up and settled in about 1692 at Knockshegowna in North Tipperary. By 1870, nine Stoney families in Tipperary owned some 5,400 acres of land between them, mostly in the area between Portumna, Birr and Roscrea.

George and Mary Stoney of Kettlewell had ten great-grandchildren who survived to adulthood. Of these James Johnston Stoney (1759–1824) and Thomas Stoney (1748–1826) are of interest. James Johnston Stoney of Oakley Park near Clareen was the grandfather of George Johnstone Stoney and Bindon Blood Stoney. Thomas Stoney of Arran Hill and Kyle Park near Borrisokane was the grandfather of several Stoney engineers.

James Johnston Stoney married Catherine Baker of Lismacue, Co. Tipperary, and had six children of whom the eldest was George (1792–1832). George Stoney in 1821 married Anne Blood of Cranagher, Co. Clare. They had four children: Anne, Katherine, George Johnstone and Bindon Blood.

The distinguished career of **George Johnstone Stoney** is described below and we have already met **Bindon Blood Stoney** in Chapter 1.

A5.2 George Johnstone Stoney FRS (1826–1911)

George Johnstone Stoney was born at Oakley Park on 15 February 1826. The family's property greatly depreciated in value after the Napoleonic wars and had to be sold. The family moved to Dublin where George entered Trinity College in 1843 and his brother Bindon in 1845. The brothers earned their fees by tutoring other students. Both graduated with distinction, George in 1848 and Bindon in 1850.

On completing his studies in physics and mathematics, Stoney became an astronomical assistant to `William Parsons, 3rd Earl of Rosse. While at Parsonstown, George prepared for Fellowship in Trinity College. He was not successful, being awarded the second Madden prize in 1851 and the first in 1852. As he could not afford to try again for Fellowship, Lord Rosse used his influence to have him appointed to the chair of Natural Philosophy at Queen's College, Galway. Stoney remained five years in Galway and stayed with his mother's half-brother, Professor William Bindon Blood. William Bindon Blood (1817–1894) trained as a civil engineer and was employed under Brunel in the construction of the Great Western Railway. He was Professor of Civil Engineering in Queen's College Galway from 1849 until 1860.

In 1857, Stoney was appointed Secretary to Queen's University of Ireland, which brought him back to Dublin. As a university administrator, Stoney devoted himself enthusiastically to improving the effectiveness of the provincial colleges in Belfast, Cork and Galway. It was, therefore, a great blow to him when the Queen's University was dissolved in 1880 and its place was taken by the Royal University, which had the power of conferring degrees purely by examination.

William Bindon Blood

Stoney was very active in the affairs of the Royal Dublin Society, serving as honorary secretary from 1871 to 1881 and as vice president from 1881 to 1911. During Stoney's tenure, the Society underwent profound changes. It handed over its great collections to the government and received capital to pursue its scientific functions and to improve Irish agriculture. Stoney and his nephew, George F. FitzGerald, played central roles in the Society's scientific meetings and discussions.

In 1863, Stoney married his cousin, Margaret Sophia, the only daughter of Robert Johnstone Stoney of Killavalla; the couple had two sons and three daughters who survived to adulthood. In spite of the death of his wife followed by two severe illnesses of his own and his heavy load of administrative duties, he still managed to carry out scientific research, often rising at five in the morning to write or to experiment before going to his office. In 1893, Stoney left Dublin to live in London, in order to give his daughters the opportunity of a university education, which was denied to them at that time in Dublin.

One of the main themes of Stoney's research was his interest in the kinetic theory of gases. In 1858, he showed that Boyle's Law is contrary to the view that the particles of a gas are at rest or that a gas can be a continuous, homogeneous substance. Ten years later, he estimated the number of molecules in a given volume of gas at normal temperature and pressure, independently of a similar estimate by Avogadro. In 1868, he considered the limitations of planetary atmospheres, correctly explaining the absence of hydrogen and helium in the Earth's atmosphere and the absence of an atmosphere on the Moon in terms of the concept of escape velocity.

Stoney introduced the word 'electron' (Greek for amber) into the scientific vocabulary. In a paper read before the British Association for the Advancement of Science in 1874, he pointed out "an absolute unit of quantity of electricity exists in that amount of it which attends each chemical bond or valency." He proposed that this quantity should be regarded as the fundamental unit of electricity and suggested the name 'electron' in 1881. In the same paper, Stoney proposed the adoption of a system of natural units of mass, length and time, based on the gravitational constant, the velocity of light and the electric charge. In 1899, physicist Max Planck proposed a similar set of units that are of significance in cosmology today. Stoney also wrote extensively about the optical theory of microscopes and telescopes, meteor showers and atomic spectra.

Stoney received many honours and distinctions during his life. Perhaps the one he valued most highly was the award of the first Boyle Medal from the Royal Dublin Society in 1899. He was elected to the Royal Society in 1861, and served as vice president (1898–99) and on its council (1898–1900). He was a member of the Royal Irish Academy and attended the meetings of the British Association for the Advancement of Science. He was a visitor to the Royal Observatory at Greenwich and to the Royal Institution, and a foreign member of the United States National Academy of Sciences. He received honorary doctorates from Queen's University of Ireland (1879) and the University of Dublin (1902). He died in London on 5 July 1911.

A5.3 The family of George Johnstone Stoney and Margaret Stoney

George Johnstone Stoney married his cousin Margaret, second daughter of Robert Johnstone Stoney of Parsonstown (Birr), and they had two sons and three daughters who survived to adulthood.

George Gerald Stoney qualified as an engineer and had a distinguished career which is described below.

Robert Bindon Stoney (1866–1914) graduated as a medical doctor from TCD in 1890. As he had tuberculosis, he tried the better climates of South Africa and Australia. He studied medicine at Sydney University and practised in New South Wales. In 1893, he married Louisa McComas and they had four children. He set up a TB sanatorium at Euchua in New South Wales. In April 1900, his cousin, George Bindon Stoney, also suffering from TB, went to Australia to be treated by him, thus re-infecting him.

Edith Anne Stoney (1869–1938) was a good mathematician coming seventeenth Wrangler in the mathematical tripos in Cambridge University in 1893, having attended Newnham College. In WWI she set up and operated X-ray equipment in a mobile hospital that moved from Troyes in France to Serbia and Greece. She was awarded the *Crois de Guerre, Médaille Epedémie* of France and the *Serbian order of St Sava*. Later, she lectured in physics at the London School of Medicine for Women.

Florence Stoney

Florence Ada Stoney OBE (1870–1932) graduated with a MB and BS from the London School of Medicine for Women and took her MD in 1898. She practised as a consultant radiologist in London and pioneered X-ray treatment at the Royal Free Hospital. After the outbreak of WWI, she organised a surgical unit and set up a field hospital in Antwerp. In March 1915, she was appointed head of the radiological department of Fulham Military Hospital. She was awarded the OBE in 1919 and the Diploma in Medical Radiology (Cambridge) in 1920. Until her retirement in 1928 she was a medical consultant in two Bournemouth hospitals.

Gertude Beatrice Stoney (1871–1955) was a sculptress. In May 1901, she went to Euchua in New South Wales to help her brother Robert care for his young family and remained in Australia for six years.

A5.4 George Gerard Stoney DSc FRS (1863–1942)

George Gerard Stoney

George Gerald Stoney, the eldest child of George Johnstone and Margaret Stoney, was born in Dublin. He studied Experimental Science in TCD and graduated with distinction in 1886. He then took an engineering degree, coming first in every subject and gaining the highest awards of the engineering school. For a year he was assistant to his uncle, Bindon Blood Stoney, Chief Engineer of the Dublin Port and Docks Board.

In 1888, he joined the firm of Clarke, Chapman & Co., Gateshead-upon-Tyne, to work with the Hon. Charles A. Parsons (1854–1931), youngest son of the 3rd Earl of Rosse and the inventor of the steam turbine. In 1884, Parsons had developed a turbine engine that he used to drive an electrical generator, thus making cheap and plentiful electricity possible.

In 1889, Parsons founded his own works at Heaton, Newcastle-upon-Tyne. At first Stoney worked as a fitter in the workshops but his previous experience of the silvering of mirrors led to his appointment in 1893 as manager of the searchlight department and foreman of the test house where turbo generators were tested under steam before delivery. Two years later he was chief designer of the steam turbine department.

In 1894, Parsons (pictured right) set up his Marine Steam Turbine Company with himself as managing director and his eldest brother, Laurence, 4th Earl of Rosse (1840–1908), as one of the five other directors. Its purpose was to apply the steam turbine to marine propulsion. Parsons decided to build an experimental vessel called *Turbinia* and Stoney supervised the design and building of the turbines for it.

In June 1887, a Naval Review was arranged at Spithead in honour of the Diamond Jubilee of Queen Victoria. All the great warships of the British Navy and several from other navies were lined up for the admiration of the Queen. Suddenly, on Saturday, 26 June, the little *Turbinia* appeared and sped between the lines of Her Majesty's ships. Rollo Appleyard reported:

> A picket-boat was put out to try to stop the intruder but the intruder was proceeding at 30 knots, against which the speed of the picket-boat was ridiculous. The picket-boat was nearly run down; her Commander took off his sword-belt and prepared to swim, the engine mast was cut in two, but the hull escaped damage.

In fact, the *Turbinia* achieved a speed of 34 knots, which was appreciably faster than the 27 knots

The *Turbinia*

the top ships of the Royal Navy were capable of. Within two years the destroyers *Viper* and *Cobra* were launched with Parsons' turbines. The first transatlantic liners to be powered by turbines were the RMS *Victorian* and *Virginian* in 1905. The first turbine-power battleship to be powered by turbines was HMS *Dreadnought* in 1906. In a few short years Parsons' steam turbines revolutionised marine propulsion. The Parsons' turbine held a near monopoly of passenger-ship propulsion during the first half of the twentieth century.

By 1910, Stoney had become technical manager of the entire Heaton works and he was elected a Fellow of the Royal Society in 1911. The firm was prospering but unfortunately a serious difference of opinion arose between Parsons and Stoney. Parsons regarded the works as his experimental workshop whereas Stoney wanted to run the plant on commercial production lines. Stoney left the company in 1912. In 1917 he was appointed Professor of Mechanical Engineering in the College of Technology in Manchester. In 1926 he returned to the Heaton works as Director of Research. He retired in 1930 and died at Heaton on 15 May 1942.

A5.5 The family of William and Anne FitzGerald

Anne Frances Stoney married William FitzGerald who later became Bishop of Cork and Cloyne and then of Killaloe. Their five surviving children were three sons, Maurice, George Francis and William, and two daughters Anne and Edith.

Anne FitzGerald became Superintendent of the City of Dublin Nursing Home.

Maurice FitzGerald (1850–1927) studied mathematics in TCD and later became Professor of Engineering at Queen's College, Belfast, from 1884 to 1910; he was interested in machines for compressing peat.

The outstanding career of **George Francis FitzGerald** is described below.

William FitzGerald became a Church of Ireland clergyman.

Edith FitzGerald married mathematician E.P. Culverwell, the first Professor of Education in TCD.

A5.6 George Francis FitzGerald FRS (1851–1901)

George Francis Fitzgerald was born in on 3 August 1851. When his father moved to Cork, George and his siblings had the good fortune to have as tutor Mary Ann Boole, the sister of mathematician George Boole (1815–1864).

FitzGerald graduated from Trinity College in 1871, at the top of his class in both mathematics and experimental physics. He spent the next six years preparing for the Fellowship examination and was successful in 1877, on his second attempt. In 1881, FitzGerald was appointed Erasmus Smith Professor of Natural and Experimental Philosophy in Trinity, holding the chair until his death.

FitzGerald's research was devoted to the development and application of Maxwell's theory of electromagnetism, first formulated in 1873. He combined MacCullagh's wave theory of light and Maxwell's equations to explain the Kerr effect in which the polarisation of light is altered on reflection from the poles of a magnet. With Oliver Lodge, Oliver Heaviside, Joseph Larmor and Heinrich Hertz, FitzGerald developed Maxwell's equations into the form we know today; the five were known as the Maxwellians.

In 1882, FitzGerald proposed a means for producing electromagnetic waves but failed to make them himself. When Hertz succeeded in this in 1888, FitzGerald brought the discovery to the attention of the British Association for the Advancement of Science, thereby ensuring its significance was appreciated. FitzGerald was elected a Fellow of the Royal Society in 1883 and was its royal medallist in 1889 for his work in theoretical physics.

In 1889 FitzGerald suggested that the failure of Michelson and Morley's 1881 experiment to detect the ether could be due to the contraction of bodies in their direction of motion.

He sent a letter to *Science* under the title '*The Ether and the Earth's Atmosphere*', which remained forgotten until 1967. Hendrik Lorentz hit upon the same idea late in 1892, and he developed it fully in conjunction with his theory of electrons. The effect is now known as the 'FitzGerald–Lorentz Contraction' and is one of the consequences of Albert Einstein's theory of relativity, which led to the concept of the ether being abandoned.

FitzGerald collaborated with W.E. Wilson who had a private observatory and laboratory at Daramona House, Co. Westmeath. In 1894 and 1896, he assisted Wilson and G.M. Minchin in making photo-electric measurements of the brightness of ten stars of first and second magnitude. In 1893, he suggested that geomagnetic storms might be due to electrified particles emitted by the Sun. He also suggested that comets' tails, aurorae, the solar corona and cathode rays were closely allied phenomena.

FitzGerald strove to improve the teaching of experimental physics in Trinity College. He obtained a disused chemical laboratory and introduced practical work into the curriculum. He was always ready to advise and encourage and three of his students went on to distinguish themselves in science: John Joly, Frederick Trouton and Thomas Preston.

Overwork eventually took its toll on his health and he died on 22 February, 1901, after an operation for a perforated ulcer. His death was a great blow to the college and the wider scientific community.

A5.7 The Descendants of Thomas Stoney of Arran Hill and Kyle Park

Thomas George Stoney married Ruth Falkiner of Mount Falcon in 1773 and they had eight children of whom the eldest, George, married Marianne Smith in 1804. Their eldest son, Thomas George, married Anna H. Waller in 1829 and they had seven children including Francis G. M. Stoney and Edward W. Stoney.

Francis Goold Morony Stoney ME (1837–97) studied engineering at Queen's College, Belfast, and was subsequently articled to Sir John Macneill, the famous railway engineer. After working at Dundalk and the Clyde, he moved abroad. While working for the Madras Navigation & Canal Company in India in the late 1860s he first became interested in sluice design. His research into the construction of completely watertight sluices resulted in the invention and patenting of the 'roller sluice' and the 'double door roller sluice'. In all, 180 sluices were built to his design, at places which included the Manchester Ship Canal, the River Rhone at Geneva, the Thames at Richmond, and the Clyde at Glasgow. He died in Germany in 1897.

Edward Waller Stoney CE CIE (1844–1931) was born in 1844. He studied engineering at Queen's College Galway where he was a scholar and gold medallist. In 1866, he went to India as an engineer on the Madras Railway, eventually rising to the position of chief engineer. He married Sarah Crawford of Cartron Abbey, Co. Longford, in 1875. He was awarded the Telford Premium in 1890–91 for his paper 'The New Chittravati Bridge'. In 1883, he invented a noiseless punkah wheel; the punkah in India was a large swinging fan fixed to the ceiling and pulled by a servant in hot weather. He died in Bournemouth in 1931.

Edward Stoney had a son, **Richard Francis Stoney CE** (1876–1963), who was chief engineer for the Public Worlds Department of Madras. He was executive engineer for the Mettur Dam Project, built in 1934 in a gorge where the river Kaveri enters the plains and provides irrigation as well as hydro-electric power.

A5.8 Alan Mathison Turing OBE FRS (1912–1954), the father of computer science

Perhaps the most remarkable of all the Stoneys was Alan Turing, grandson of Edward W. Stoney. Although born in England, Alan Turing's ancestors were Irish and Scottish.

Edward W. Stoney had two sons and two daughters. All four were sent back to their home country for their education, in this case to their uncle, William Crawford, a bank manager in Co Clare. The Crawfords moved to Dublin in 1891. The younger daughter Ethel married Julius Turing in St Batholomew's Church, Dublin, on 1 October 1907.

Julius Turing had been born in Nottinghamshire and had joined the Indian Civil Service, rising after ten years to the level of head assistant collector and magistrate.

Julius and Ethel Turing returned to India and their first son, John, was born on 1 September 1908. Their second son, Alan, was born on 23 June 1912 in London while his father was on leave. Ethel stayed on in England until September 1913 and then left the boys in the care of a retired Army couple, Colonel and Mrs Ward, in St Leonards-on-Sea. The parents visited the boys whenever they could but it was not a happy childhood.

Alan was educated at Hazelhurst School, then Sherborne School in Dorset. He won an open scholarship in Mathematics to King's College, Cambridge, and matriculated in 1931. He graduated in 1934 with distinction and was awarded a Fellowship in 1935. It was at Cambridge that he developed the proof that states that automatic computation cannot solve all mathematical problems. This concept, also known as the Turing machine, is considered the basis for the modern theory of computation. Next, he spent two years as a Visiting Fellow at Princeton University. In 1936, his paper *On Computable Numbers* was completed.

Alan returned to King's College in 1938. When WWII broke out, he joined the Government Code and Cypher School at Bletchley Park, Buckinghamshire, where he played a vital role in deciphering the messages encrypted by the German Enigma machine, which provided vital intelligence for the Allies. He led a team that designed an electro-mechanical machine known as a 'bombe' that successfully decoded German messages.

The high-level intelligence produced at Bletchley Park, codenamed Ultra, provided crucial assistance to the Allied war effort. General Eisenhower, Supreme Allied Commander in Europe, said that the decoding successes at Bletchley Park shortened the war by at least two years, saving many thousands of lives. Turing was awarded an OBE in 1946 for his contributions but his work remained secret for many years.

After the War, Turing went to the National Physical Laboratory where he presented the first detailed design for a stored-programme computer – the Automatic Computing Engine (ACE). Although ACE was feasible, the secrecy surrounding the wartime work at Bletchley Park led to delays and he became disillusioned. In late 1947, he returned to Cambridge for a sabbatical year during which the Pilot ACE was being built in his absence; it ran its first programme in May 1950.

In 1948, he was appointed Reader in the Mathematics Department of Manchester University. A year later he became Deputy Director of the Computing Laboratory and developed software for the Manchester Mark 1 Computer. Turing also addressed the problem of artificial intelligence and proposed an experiment, which became known as the Turing test, an attempt to define a standard for a machine to be called 'intelligent'. The idea was that a computer could be said to 'think' if a human interrogator could not tell it apart, through conversation, from a human being. He was elected a Fellow of the Royal Society in 1951.

From 1952 onwards Turing worked on mathematical biology, in particular the biological processes that cause an organism to develop its shape. He used reaction-diffusion equations, which are central to the field of pattern formation. His contribution is considered a seminal piece of work in this field.

In 1952, Turing was arrested and tried for homosexuality, then a criminal offence. To avoid prison, he accepted hormone injections. In that era, people who were homosexual were considered a security risk as they were open to blackmail. Turing's security clearance was withdrawn, meaning he could no longer work for GCHQ, the post-war successor to Bletchley Park.

He was found by his cleaner on 8 June 1954. He had died the day before of cyanide poisoning, a half-eaten apple beside his bed. The coroner's verdict was suicide. He was only 42 years of age.

In 1998, Sir Roger Penrose, then Professor of Mathematics at the University of Oxford, wrote:

> This century has witnessed several revolutions in scientific thought and in technology. Relativity, quantum mechanics, antibiotics, genetics, aeroplanes and television are some obvious examples. As the century draws to its close, however, it is another revolution that is now beginning to make the most profound mark on almost every aspect of our lives. This is the general-purpose computer. The central seminal figure in this computer revolution was Alan Turing, whose outstanding originality and vision was what made it possible, in work originating in the mid-1930s. Although it is now hard to see what the limits of the computer revolution might eventually be, it was Turing himself who pointed out to us the very existence of such theoretical limitations.

These issues raise pivotal philosophical questions, which will, I am sure, be argued about for centuries to come. Turing was, indeed, a deep and influential philosopher in addition to his having made contributions to mathematics, technology and code-breaking that profoundly contribute to our present-day wellbeing.

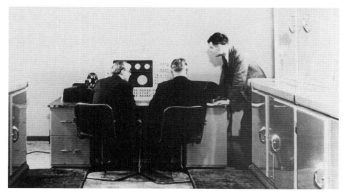

Turing at the Ferranti Mark I computer in 1951

APPENDIX 6

THE
DUBLIN PENNY JOURNAL

CONDUCTED BY P. DIXON HARDY, M.R.I.A.
Vol. IV.   AUGUST 15, 1835 No. 163.

The learned and munificent Provost of Trinity College, Dublin, Doctor Francis Andrews, having bequeathed to the College £3000, and £250 per annum, towards the building of an Observatory, and furnishing it with proper instruments, which sum was to arise from an accumulation of a part of his property, to commence upon a particular contingency happening in his family, the College, to hasten the execution of the plan, advanced from their own funds a sum considerably exceeding the original bequest; and having elected the Rev. H. Ussher as Professor, sent him to England to order from Mr. Ramsden the best in-struments, without limitation of price. Those ordered were, a transit instrument of four feet axis, and six feet focal length, bearing four inches and a quarter aperture, with different magnifying powers; an entire circle of ten feet diameter, moveable on a vertical axis, for measuring altitudes; an equatorial instrument, the circles being five feet diameter; and an achromatic telescope, mounted on a polar axis, and carried by an heliostatic movement, for occasional observations.

The transit instrument arrived as ordered, while Dr. Ussher was Professor; but the great circle for altitudes was not sent from London till many years afterwards, in the time of his successor, the Rev. Dr. Brinkley, now Bishop of Cloyne, who made with it his observations upon the parallax of the fixed stars. This circle was begun, as ordered, with a diameter of ten feet; but was reduced by Ramsden to nine feet, and afterwards to eight feet, of which last size it was finished by Ramsden's successor, Berge. Only one other astronomical circle, so large as this, has been ever made, namely, that which was finished for Cambridge a few years ago, but which is not capable of moving in azimuth like the Dublin circle. The two remaining instruments, ordered by Dr. Ussher, were never sent from London; but the late Christopher Sharp of Dublin, had almost completed before he died, an equatorial instrument with heliostatic movement, conceived and executed in a style which does great honor to his memory. This instrument carries an achromatic telescope, furnished by Cauchoix of Paris, of which the object-glass is composed of a convex quartz, and a concave flint lens, and exceeds five inches in aperture. The Observatory possesses also an excellent achromatic telescope by Dollond, and clocks by Arnold and Sharp.

The next point to be considered was the arrangement of the building, and the most commodious disposition of the instruments, so as to give to each a situation justly suited to the particular observations to be made. With-out loss of time, the Observatory was erected on Dunsink Hill, about four miles north-west of Dublin Castle, and about seventy yards above the level of the sea. It is founded on a solid rock of limestone of some miles extent, which, near the Observatory, rises to within six inches of the surface. The horizon is remarkably extensive, without the smallest interruption on any side, except that on the south the Wicklow mountains, distant about fifteen English miles, rise about a degree and a half.

To give any thing like a correct idea of this building would occupy far more space than we could allocate to the subject. We shall merely notice a few particulars. It is a handsome building, presenting in front a facade of two wings, and a projecting centre, crowned by a dome. Besides apartments for the professor, there are two rooms particularly appropriated to astronomical purposes—the Equatorial and Meridian rooms. The former is immediately beneath the dome, which is intersected by an aperture of two feet six inches in breadth, and is moveable by means of rackwork, so that the aperture may be directed to any point of the horizon. The equatorial instrument rests on a solid pillar of substantial masonry, sixteen feet square. The Meridian room of the west side of the building, is thirty-seven feet two inches long, and twenty-three feet broad in the inside clear, and twenty-one feet high. It contains the transit instrument, and the celebrated eighty-feet[sic] Astronomical Circle. The pillars of the transit instrument—which stand on a solid block of Portland stone, nine feet two inches in length, by three feet in breadth, and sixteen inches thick—are seven feet six inches high, their bases three feet from north to south, and two feet six inches from east to west. Each of the supporting pillars consisting of one solid piece, all effects of mortar and cement arc avoided, and what is of more importance, all iron cramps are unnecessary. The temperature of the pillars at different heights is shown by thermometers, the tubes of which are bent at right angles, and their bulbs arc inserted into the stone, and surrounded with dust of the same stone.

We need scarcely mention that the Professor who now fills the situation with so much honour to himself and the College is William Rowan Hamilton, Esq. Royal Astronomer of Ireland.

The Observatory commands on the south side a fine view of the surrounding country, with a gentle declivity to the river, and from thence a varied picture of the rich scenery of the woods of the Phoenix Park, terminated in the back-ground by the majestic grandeur of the Wicklow mountains. To the south east lies the city of Dublin, distant four miles, the semi-circular bay with its shipping, and the great South Wall, extending five miles into the sea, and terminated by the Light-house; the new piers forming Kingstown harbour; the ridge of rocky hills, called The Three Brothers forming the head of Dalkey, and bearing Malpas's Obelisk on the highest point. On the east and north-east Clontarf and its environs, the Hill of Howth, Ireland's Eye, and Lambay. From thence to the north-west the prospect is so uncommonly level and extensive as to gratify the astronomer much more than the painter; but even this variety is not without its beauty. To the south-west are the ruins at Castleknock; and to the west, the extended and rich view of Kildare, in which Mr. Connolly's Obelisk forms a grand and central object.

Bibliography

Ball 1895: *Great Astronomers* by Sir Robert Stawell Ball, Isbister, London, pp 303-334

Ball 1915: *Reminiscences and Letters of Sir Robert Ball*, Edited by his son, W. Valentine Ball, Cassell & Co., London, pp xiv + 406

Bennett 1990: *Church, State and Astronomy in Ireland – 200 Years of Armagh Observatory*, by James Bennett, Armagh Observatory, Armagh, pp vi + 277

Bunbury 2009: *Dublin Docklands – An Urban Voyage* by Turtle Bunbury, Montague Publications Group, Dublin, 2009, pp 251

Burnett 1989a: *"Vulgar and Mechanick" – The Scientific Instrument Trade in Ireland 1650–1921*, by John Burnett & Alison Morrison-Low, National Museums of Scotland and Royal Dublin Society, Edinburgh and Dublin, pp ix + 166

Cooke 1992: *John Hutton & Sons, Summerhill, Dublin, Coachbuilders 1779–1925* in *Dublin Historical Review*, Vol. 45, No. 1 (Spring 1992), pp 11-27

Copeland 2006: *Colossus: The Secrets of Bletchley Park's Codebreaking Computers,* ed. B. Jack Copeland, Oxford University Press, pp xvi + 462

Corcoran 2000: *Through Streets Broad and Narrow – A history of Dublin Trams,* By Michael Corcoran, Midland Publishing, pp 160

Cox 1998: *Civil Engineering Heritage, Ireland*, by R.C. Cox & M.H. Gould, The Institution of Engineers of Ireland, Dublin, pp vii + 296

De Courcy 1996: *The Liffey in Dublin* by John W. de Courcy, Gill & Macmillan, pp xlii + 468

Friendly 1977: *Beaufort of the Admiralty – The Life of Sir Francis Beaufort 1774–1857*, by Alfred Friendly, Hutchinson, London (American Edition, Random House, New York), pp 362

Gilligan 1988: *A History of the Port of Dublin,* by Henry A. Gilligan, Gill and Macmillan, pp xvi + 293

Hankins 1980: *Sir William Rowan Hamilton*, by Thomas Hankins, John Hopkins University Press, Baltimore, pp xxi + 474

Hodges 1983: *Alan Turing: The Enigma of Intelligence*, by Andrew Hodges, Burnett Books, London, pp 586

King 1955: *The History of the Telescope*, by Henry C. King, Dover, 1979, pp xvi + 256

McConnell 2013: *Jesse Ramsden: the craftsman who believed that big was beautiful,* by Anita McConnell, in *The Antiquarian Astronomer*, Issue 7, March 2013, pp 41-53

McGovern 2013: *A Mystic Dream of 4*, by Iggy McGovern, Quaternia Press, pp 92

Mollan 1995: *Irish National Inventory of Historic Scientific Instruments*, by Charles Mollan, Samton Ltd., pp 501

Mollan 2002: *Irish Innovators in Science and Technology*, Edited by Charles Mollan, Brendan Finucane & William Davis, Royal Irish Academy & Enterprise Ireland, Dublin, pp xvi + 256

Mollan 2007: *It's Part of What We Are: some Irish contributors to the development of the chemical and physical sciences Vol. 2*, by Charles Mollan, Royal Dublin Society, Dublin, pp xli + 1770

National Library 2003: *For the Safety of All – Images and Inspections of Irish Lighthouses*, with text by Brendan O'Donoghue, Mel Boyd & Michael Farrelly, National Library of Ireland, Dublin, pp 92

Nicholson 1988: *The Ulysses Guide – Tours through Joyce's Dublin,* by Robert Nicholson, Menthuen, London, x + pp 150

O'Byrne 1849: *A Naval Biographical Dictionary: comprising the life and services of every living officer in Her Majesty's Navy, from the rank of Admiral of the Fleet to that of Lieutenant inclusive,* by William R O'Byrne, Naval & Military Press, UK, 2005, pp 1400

Ó Cionnaith 2010: *Mapping, Measurement and Metropolis – How Land Surveyors shaped Eighteenth-Century Dublin,* Four Courts Press, Dublin, pp xxiv + 246

Purser 2004: *Jellett, O'Brien, Purser and Stokes – Seven Generations, Four Families*, by Michael Purser, Prejmer Verlag, Dublin, pp 240

Ryder 2010: *An Irishman of Note – George Johnstone Stoney*, by Adrian J. Ryder, NUIG, Galway, pp 119. [Online] http://ajryder.com/wpcontent/uploads/2012/05/stoney.pdf.

Scaife 2000: *From Galaxies to Turbines, Science, Technology and the Parsons Family*, by W. Garrett Scaife, Institute of Physics Publishing, Bristol and Philadelphia, pp xvi + 579

Sobel 1984: *Longitude: The True Story of a Lone Genius Who Solved the Greatest Scientific Problem of His Time*, by Dava Sobel, Fourth Estate, London, viii + pp 184

Steel 2000: *Marking Time – The Epic Quest to Invent the Perfect Calendar,* by Duncan Steel, John Wiley & Sons, New York, pp ix + 422

Steinicke 2010: *Observing and Cataloguing Nebulae and Star Clusters - from Herschel to Dreyer's New General Catalogue*, by Wolfgang Steinicke, Cambridge University Press, UK, pp 660

Stoney 1879: *Some Old Annals of the Stoney Family*, compiled by F.S. Stoney, Maclure and Maconald, London, pp 76. [Online] https://search.ancestry.com/search/db.aspx?dbid=24937

Stoney 2008: *Some Newer Annals of the Stoney Family*, edited by Alex B.M. Stoney, astoney@ozemail.com.au, Australia, pp 265. [Online] https://catalogue.nla.gov.au/Record/385520

Turing 2010: *Alan M. Turing: Centenary Edition* by Sara Turing, Cambridge University Press, pp xiv + 169

United Nations Conference on Trade and Development 2020: *Trade and Development Report 2020 From Global Pandemic to Prosperity for All: Avoiding another lost decade.* United Nations Publications. New York. pp139

Wayman 1987: *Dunsink Observatory, 1785–1985, A Bicentennial History*, by Patrick A. Wayman, Dublin Institute for Advanced Studies & Royal Dublin Society, Dublin, pp xiii + 353

Wayman 1972: *Notes on the History of Dunsink Observatory III: The Arnold Clocks* in *The Irish Astronomical Journal*, Vol. 10, pp 275–281. [Online] http://adsabs.harvard.edu/full/1972IrAJ...10..275W (accessed Sep. 2013)

Wayman 1887: *Dunsink Clock Control System from 1874* in *The Irish Astronomical Journal,* Vol 18. pp 23-27. [Online] http://articles.adsabs.harvard.edu/full/1987IrAJ...18...23W (accessed Sep. 2013)

Weaire 2009: *George Francis FitzGerald,* edited by Denis Weaire, Living Edition, Austria, pp viii + 148

Whitesell 1998: *A Creation of His Own: Tappan's Detroit Observatory*, by Patricia S. Whitesell, University of Michigan, Ann Arbor, pp xx +236.

Index

Page numbers in italics refer to images